SpringerBriefs in Accounting

More information about this series at http://www.springer.com/series/11900

Adriana Bruno

New Public Management (NPM) and the Introduction of an Accrual Accounting System

A Case Study of an Italian Regional Government Authority

Springer

Adriana Bruno
Economics and Management
University of Ferrara
Ferrara, Italy

ISSN 2196-7873 ISSN 2196-7881 (electronic)
SpringerBriefs in Accounting
ISBN 978-3-030-57385-0 ISBN 978-3-030-57386-7 (eBook)
https://doi.org/10.1007/978-3-030-57386-7

This Springer imprint is published by the registered company Springer Nature Switzerland AG
The registered company address is: Gewerbestrasse 11, 6330 Cham, Switzerland

A mio figlio Costantino

Acknowledgements

Writing a book is not one individual's work, rather it involves several people who contribute to the process in different ways. Therefore, I acknowledge the efforts of multiple people, specifically, Prof. Irvine Lapsley for his guidance throughout this whole process; a special thanks for his hospitality during my unforgettable 6 months of visiting study research at the Institute of Public Sector Accounting in Edinburgh, and moreover, Profs. Riccardo Mussari and Paolo Ricci who guided me in my academic path. Finally, I would like to thank the Campania Region who offered me the opportunity to collect the data as a non-participant observer.

About This Book

The adoption of accrual accounting is seen as self-evident by NPM advocates (Lapsley et al. 2009). Most accrual accounting studies are ex post studies. This research analyzes the initial stage of development of an accrual accounting system as the *emergence of new technologies* (Latour 1987). This study contributes to understand the complexity of apparently neutral tools involved in a Public Sector reform. This research reveals the emergence of an accrual accounting system that relates to technical, managerial, and political influences. The research site is in Italy, a country where the process of reform is underway across the whole government. The study setting for this research is the intermediate level of government (the regional level) where a trial period was underway. The data for this study was collected in several ways: compiling and analyzing law and key policy documents; moreover, the discussions which took place through video call conversations in a region in the trial are analyzed. The evidence collected to date reveals an absence of a well-defined template for the implementation of accrual accounting in government.

Contents

About the Author

Adriana Bruno is Ph.D. in Public Management, University of Salerno Italy. She is Research Fellow in Public Management at the Department of Economics and Management of the University of Ferrara (Italy). Her academic interests are in the field of management, governance, accounting, and performance measurement, especially in the public sector.

List of Figures

List of Tables

Chapter 1
Introduction

In recent decades, the dissemination and the adoption of New Public Management (NPM) has been significant within the new public sector (Hood, 1991, 1995). The New Public Management is a model that privileges "quantification", often by adopting managerial instruments from the private sector. Indeed, the main points of NPM could be summarized as a replication of private sector practices which focus on quantification, especially in accounting (Olson et al., 1998). One such key innovation is the adoption of accrual accounting from business enterprise. The debates about the adoption of accrual accounting and financial reporting techniques by the public sector have been widespread over the last decade.

Accrual-based systems are not necessarily consistent with public entities. Many scholars have discussed the (in)appropriateness of accrual-based accounting systems, as an alternative to cash-based or obligation-based systems (Pollit & Bouckaert, 2004; Broadbent & Guthrie, 2008). Conversely, some note that cash-based accounting does not allow the government to obtain all necessary information regarding liabilities and potential benefits related to investments (Christensen & Parker, 2010). Thus, the study of accrual accounting by governments is a challenging topic for researchers.

In the literature on accrual accounting in the public sector, it is possible to distinguish at least two main opposing streams of thought. The first of these reflects questions as to "*why the adoption is desirable*". These studies underline the benefits and uses of information in terms of managerial effectiveness from the move to accrual accounting (Hyndman & Connolly, 2011; Ryan, 1998). So, proponents of public sector reform depict bundles of techniques as politically *neutral mechanisms* for enhancing strategic decision-making and for improved efficiency in evaluating performance and service costs (Guthrie, 1998). Also, most accrual accounting studies are ex post studies. However, recently, the debate about accrual accounting has shifted onto discussion of implementation issues. Thus, the second stream of thinking on this topic ponders questions pertaining to the "*complexity*" in the translation of the accrual-based methodologies adopted by private sector organizations into public

A. Bruno, *New Public Management (NPM) and the Introduction of an Accrual Accounting System*, SpringerBriefs in Accounting,
https://doi.org/10.1007/978-3-030-57386-7_1

sector agencies (Caccia & Steccolini, 2006; Lapsley & Wright, 2004; Broadbent & Guthrie, 2008). This research is located in this second stream of writing on accrual accounting in the public sector.

A literature review of NPM reveals that accrual accounting is depicted as self-evident in New Public Management literature (Lapsley et al., 2009). However, it is problematic in its implementation. After several years of this reform, the unresolved question is: what does accrual accounting mean in practice for government? For the majority of cases, our current knowledge is based on ex post studies. That is why we focus in this study on the emergence of a system to enrich our understanding of what accrual accounting means in practice for government. This research analyzes the initial stage of development of an accrual accounting system. The research site is in Italy, a country where a process of reform is underway across the whole government (Legislative Decree n. 118/2011). This research has focused on the specific context of regional government, which also offers distinctive evidence because it has been neglected by the extant national (Ricci, 2005; Caperchione, 2008) and international (Broadbent and Guthrie, 2008; Jagalla et al., 2011) literature.

This research is largely informed by the *social construction of science studies*, whose most eminent scholar is Latour (1979, 2013). Indeed, in science and technology studies there is a body of social studies that focuses on the creation of scientific facts and examines how the scientists interact to produce accepted technologies: the "social construction of technology" (SCOT). This research analyzes the initial stage of development of an accrual accounting system as the *emergence of new technologies* (Latour, 1987). Policy documents are the text by which government reform takes place. Adopting this framework (policy as a blueprint), the analysis of relevant policy documents facilitates the capture of the meaning of accrual accounting and enhances understanding of how the process of reform takes place. Before analyzing the shaping of accrual accounting in the public sector, it is necessary to understand the meaning of accounting and to focus our attention on the analysis of two key elements behind a government process of reform: the first one is the policy documents by which the reform is disclosed; the second one is the networking of institutional actors behind the text and controversies between key institutional players, the policy-makers.

The study setting for this research is the regional level of government (Campania region) where a trial period is underway. This work aims to participate in the debate on the effects of the decision to adopt accrual accounting in government, particularly in regional bodies. Campania is a region in the South of Italy where accrual accounting has not yet been implemented. Thus, the experimental introduction of accrual accounting in regional government offers an exceptional opportunity to study the manner by which such systems are enacted, *constructed*, and *fabricated* (Preston et al., 1992). The data for this study was collected in several ways: compiling and analyzing law, key policy documents, and the discussions which took place through video conversations in a region in the trial.

The main result of this research is that the adoption of accrual accounting is seen as self-evident by NPM advocates (Lapsley et al., 2009). However, the evidence collected to date reveals the absence of a well-defined template for the implementation of accrual accounting in government. In particular, problematic aspects in some technical issues are the interpretation and fabrications related to the shaping of the standard, the identification of administrative phenomena on an accrual basis, the introduction of new procedures to carry out the process, and adaption of the structure for managing new information flows. This study contributes to understand the complexity of apparently neutral tools involved in a Public Sector reform. This research reveals the emergence of an accrual accounting system that relates to technical, managerial, and political influence.

Accrual accounting implementation in central government has been studied in many countries with similar findings of difficulties in detecting effective systems in use. More recent studies of accrual accounting in Australia highlight the significant role of management consultants as interpreters of what accrual accounting is, or should be, the authors talked about a *phantom image* of accrual accounting (Christensen and Parker, 2010). A recent study reveals that the reform in UK-established accounting practice was reshaped by the adopters of accrual accounting, but the subsequent practices were still very different from private sector practice. The policy outcome is defined as "*accounting mutations*" (Lapsley, 2012). This work aims to participate in the debate on the effects of the decision to adopt accrual accounting in government, particularly in regional bodies. In the past, this perspective has been deployed in studies of accounting in action (Miller & O'Leary, 1990; Robson, 1992; Preston et al., 1992).

The book is organized as follows:

- Chapter 2 presents a literature review: prior research on accrual accounting as a public sector reform;
- Chapter 3 describes the theoretical framework used—accounting as a technology—is elaborated upon.
- Chapter 4 shows the research design—the study setting, sources of information, and the analysis of data—which is set out.
- Chapters 5 and 6 contain the research results. This chapter is organized into two sections: an overall perspective on the reform based on a documentary analysis and then this is complemented with empirical evidence from the case study.

Chapter 2
Prior Research on Accrual Accounting as a Public Sector Reform

Abstract In this section, we reviewed the academic debate related to the introduction of accrual accounting in central and local governments at the international level. A systematic analysis of 20 years of accrual accounting research has been conducted. First, this section presents an overview of the reforms implemented in many countries as a consequence of the diffusion of New Public Management paradigm. One of the key elements in this process is the implementation of accrual accounting in government. Accrual accounting involves different issues related to political studies, accounting, organizational, planning, and control. As a consequence, each paper written on the subject of accrual accounting appears to be very complex and difficult to summarize. Scholars have different approaches to the accrual accounting implementation and investigate several topics related to different sectors. The critical lens chosen for retracing these studies is the *research approach* adopted by authors, *ex post* or *ex ante*. This kind of classification may be useful to better define the theoretical contribution of the scholars and the main contribution of this research. This section, at its conclusion, will also discuss gaps in the existing literature, and it outlines the main contribution of this research. Moreover, it will explain the research questions and the direction of the study.

2.1 New Public Management and Accrual Accounting Studies: An Overview

In recent decades, the dissemination and the adoption of New Public Management (NPM) ideas has been significant within the new public sector (Hood, 1991, 1995). New Public Management is a model that privileges "quantification", often by adopting managerial instruments from the business sector. One such key innovation is the adoption of accrual accounting from business enterprise (Olson et al., 1998).

Accrual accounting is an accounting practice under which transactions and other events are recognized when they occur, and not only when cash or its equivalent is received or paid. Accrual accounting is seen as a key instrument for reducing the cost of public services because it increases transparency by identifying and measuring

A. Bruno, *New Public Management (NPM) and the Introduction of an Accrual Accounting System*, SpringerBriefs in Accounting,
https://doi.org/10.1007/978-3-030-57386-7_2

all assets and liabilities. This may improve the public management decision-making processes and public accountability (Chan, 2003; Likierman, 1992).

The introduction of accrual accounting may also make it easier to compare the cost of public provisions with the costs of services purchased directly from non-governmental sources (Newberry & Pallot, 2005). It is generally expected that accrual accounting should help to identify the full cost of activities. This enables improved decision-making when it comes to resource allocation, coordination, and control (Likierman, 2000). Moreover, better decision-making should, in turn, enhance performance. Pressure to improve accountability, transparency, and control over resources has made accrual accounting as an essential component of government modernization. Many countries have carried out reforms to their accounting systems by introducing accrual accounting (Chan, 2003). Most of the New Public Management literature has studied the move from cash to accrual-based accounting by covering the process in individual countries.

The debates about the adoption of accrual accounting and financial reporting techniques by the public sector have been widespread over the last decade. Many scholars have discussed the appropriateness of accrual-based accounting systems, as an alternative to cash-based or obligation-based systems. Accrual-based systems are not necessarily consistent with Public entities. Conversely, some note that cash-based accounting does not allow the government to obtain all necessary information regarding liabilities and potential benefits related to investments (Christensen & Parker, 2010). Thus, the study of accrual accounting by governments is challenging for researchers.

In the literature on accrual accounting in the public sector, it is possible to distinguish at least two opposing schools of thought. The first of these asks, "*Why is the adoption desirable?*" These studies underline the limitations to use the information provided through accrual accounting to improve managerial effectiveness (Hyndman & Connolly, 2011; Ryan, 1998). Proponents of public sector reform depict bundles of techniques as politically *neutral mechanisms* for enhancing strategic decision-making and for improved efficiency in evaluating performance and service costs (Guthrie, 1998). However, recently, the debate about accrual accounting has shifted to focus on implementation issues. The second school of thought ponders how to translate accrual-based methodologies adopted by private sector organizations into public sector agencies. This research is located in this stream.

In literature, the *complexity* of accrual accounting implementation in governments has been investigated in many countries and from different points of view. For instance, the Federation des Experts Comptables Européens argued that accrual accounting may provide better support for planning and managing resources and more generally, for decision-making processes. This, they argue, allows for greater comparability, even between different entities. The International Public Sector Accounting Standards Board (IPSASB) has issued accounting standards to Public Administrations, inspired by International Financial Reporting Standards (IAS/IFRS). However, some studies have observed that many governments do not "tolerate" the International Public Sector Accounting Standards well (Anselmi & Ponzo, 2009; Christiaens & Reyniers, 2009; Pina et al., 2009). Other studies focus on technical issues related to the difficulty of quantifying particular kinds of "goods", such as heritage assets (Barton, 1999; Carnegie & Wolnizer, 1996; Mautz, 1988). These authors have asserted that accrual accounting is not sector neutral and also contend that it is a method designed for the commercial sector that cannot be imported to the public sector without modification. They claim that accrual accounting reveals problems when accounting for heritage and similar assets, like monuments, reserves, parks, roads, and other social, cultural, and scientific assets. In literature, there is also evidence of limited use of accrual accounting information by politicians (Paulsson, 2006).

2.2 Accrual Accounting for Government: What It Means in Practice

There are special issues related to accrual accounting for government, which make it a very complicated matter in practice. One of them relates to the adoption of international standards, IPSAS.

The literature has developed into considerable detail regarding the adoption of IPSAS in public entities, the main issues have been the accountability function, the information function, and the needs of information of its users. The IPSAS are internationally recognized as accrual-based public sectors reporting standards, and these are mainly related to financial statements and financial reporting.

The IPSASB plays a key international role in the development of IPSAS and in the diffusion of recommended practice guidelines. Many accountancy professions and academics are involved in the board, and strong link has been established with IFAC. In fact, the IPSAS are referred by the IFAC; however, the IPSASB is an independent board. The development of IPSAS comes from IFRS, and these are the private sector equivalent. The implementation of accrual accounting methodologies and the adoption of IPSAS attract scholars from private and public sectors. The Anglo-Saxon countries are most "IPSAS-oriented"; however, recent studies show that even continental countries such as Spain, Portugal, and Austria are toward IPSAS. The question is "Why is it not so easy to adopt standards in practice?" Because individual sets of accounting standards are able to develop practical solutions, this issue will be clearly shown in Chap. 6.

Another most relevant accrual accounting issues are related to heritage assets, infrastructure assets, and non-exchange transactions. Heritage assets are land and buildings of historical importance. Sometimes referred to as public domain assets or patrimony, they are highly prized, often irreplaceable, enjoyed by all—sometimes all the world—though the government has the duty to preserve and maintain them. Accounting requires the financial statements of any organization to be comprehensive, reporting on all revenues, expenses, assets, liabilities and cash flows, not selections from them, and accounting standards define what is meant by this comprehensiveness. Accounting defines these items as assets and therefore requires them to be included in the balance sheet and, when relevant, a related depreciation charge to be made in the operating statement. The valuation of heritage assets is controversial in theory and in practice, as is shown in Chap. 6, because the historical costs are not available and the fair value could be not determinated.

In the same way, infrastructure assets are assets such as water, lake, roads, and bridges; these assets can have a very long life. As with other tangible fixed assets, they are generally recognized in the balance sheet and valued in financial terms. The specific issue that they raise is the treatment of depreciation. Also, this issue is fully addressed in Chap. 6.

2.3 NPM Reforms: A Brief Country Overview

In most countries, the initial effort to adopt accrual accounting has been undertaken by local government (Broadbent & Guthrie, 2008; Jagalla et al., 2011). A report by IFAC in 2000 identified the countries that had adopted accrual accounting in central and local government (IFAC, 2000). In many cases, accrual accounting in local government was introduced in countries with well-established accounting professions. However, the major focus of this study is on central government, specifically a regional government, which presents its own set of problems for policy-makers. This research focuses on the specific context of regional government and also offers distinctive evidence, because regional government has been neglected by the existing national (Caperchione, 2012) and international literature (Broadbent & Guthrie, 2008; Jagalla et al., 2011).

There are two large collections of studies related to the European Countries. These include a book edited by Pricewaterhouse Coopers in 2003, "Reforming governmental accounting and budgeting in Europe", which presents an overview of reforms in European Countries adopting a contingency perspective (Lüder & Jones, 2003). Recently, Ernst & Young presented a new overview and comparison of public accounting and auditing practices among the 27 EU Member States (Ernst & Young, 2012).

The greatest experience in accrual accounting implementation in central government can be observed in *Australia* and in *New Zealand.* The implementation in those countries began in 1980. The European country identified as high-intensity adopter of NPM ideas (Hood, 1995) is the *United Kingdom.* In *Australia,* in the State of New South Wales, government officials have reported inertia and public sector resistance to change since 1992 (Guthrie, 1998; Carlin, 2005). *New Zealand* is one of the earliest adopters of accrual accounting in central government, in that country may have resulted in an erosion of the assets held by the central government (Newberry & Pallot, 2004). The *UK* was also at the forefront of the adopters of accrual accounting for government. However, studies of this reform reveal that those implementing the accounting practice lacked necessary expertise (Connolly & Hyndman, 2006).

In other words, it is still true that one of the benefits of accrual accounting is that it provides more complete information to improve decision-making. As a consequence, the accrual accounting system has been depicted as an instrument to bring about useful to change in the managerial approach to managing public administrators. However, more recent studies of accrual accounting in Australia highlight the significant role of management consultants to interpret what accrual accounting is, or should be (Christensen & Parker, 2010). The same thought is expressed by Clarke, in Australia "accrual accounting was received with approbation naturally by the accounting profession" (Clarke, 2012). Frank Clarke in 2012 advises that it is important to not confuse the management efficiency system with the accounting system. Specifically, the author warns not to fall into the illusion that reforming the accounting system will automatically lead to improvements in management efficiency (Clarke, 2012). In the same way, a recent study by Newberry about New Zealand confirms the influence of consultants in transforming budget and financial reporting of the State of New Zealand Incorporated (Carosi, 2012, p. 6; Newberry, 2012).

Moreover, the latest study by Lapsley reveals that the reform in the UK-established accounting practice was reshaped by the adopters of accrual accounting. But the subsequent practices were still very different from private sector practice. The study describes the story of the adoption of accrual accounting in central and local governments in the UK, showing that the reform was more complex than a simple statement. During this process, there were significant divergences from private sector practice and at the same time, these changes differed from previous practice. The policy outcome is defined as "*accounting mutations*" (Lapsley, 2012). Moreover, there is evidence of a limited use of this information by elected members of Parliament (Connolly & Hyndman, 2011; Ezzamel et al., 2013).

However, there have been conflicts and *non-compliance* with these new accounting regimes in local government. The study by Christiaens and Van Peteghem in 2007 aims to explain these issues by using a *compliance index* when examining implementation of accounting reforms in *Flemish municipalities*. The Compliance Index quantifies the degree of implementation with the adapted elements required by the legislator. It contains technical variable elements included in the private sector accounting and transparency components, elements typically related to the NPM context. This is a longitudinal study which shows that the implementation of governmental reforms does not appear to be self-regulated and after some years many problems still occur. There was also a lack of authority by the standard-setting body. Looking at the different components of compliance, the authors underlined that the accrual accounting system, together with specific rules for the registration of transactions, have been transferred without any further information regarding the integration of the budgetary accounting into the new accounting system (Christiaens & Van Peteghem, 2007, p. 394).

The implementation difficulties regarding accrual accounting extend to key concepts, such as *materiality*. In a study of the Norwegian central government, there were major difficulties over the precise determination of this concept (Nesbakk & Mellemvik, 2011). In that research is described the complexity of the accrual accounting implementation in central government, on this basis, the study is focused on the ways in which various factors and actors were involved in the construction of materiality. Specifically, the issue of *discretion* in the implementation is illustrated (Nesbakk & Mellemvik, 2011, p. 213).

The last debates have revealed accrual accounting as a *fluid technique* in terms of *its non-neutrality*. There have been conflicts and *non-compliance* with new accounting regimes in local government (Christiaens & Van Peteghem, 2007). There is also evidence of *ambiguity* in the adoption of accrual accounting information, which was not used well by elected politicians or by public service managers in local government (Arnaboldi & Lapsley, 2009). Specifically, this study reveals conflict and ambiguity in the implementation of accrual accounting. It shows the failure of a top-down rationalistic approach of policy implementation. Secondly, it argued the *symbolic interpretation* of accounting in practice.

Looking at national literature, the Italian approach to study the implementation of accrual accounting in government has been characterized by a lack of empirical studies (Nasi and Steccolini, 2008, p. 176). Some Italian authors have revealed that reforms in public sector accounting were legally prescriptive and based on a top-down approach (Caperchione, 2003). There are events that characterized the process of change, which is often caused by resistance (Caccia & Steccolini, 2006), including the symbolic and non-real existent role of the reforms (Caperchione, 2012). The changes in Italy took place in most cases without true understanding of the reasons and the opportunity for change (Ricci, 2012b).

Recently, some researchers have also discussed the lack of precision and the high level of discretionary practices that accrual accounting implementation brings. Sometimes, this aspect is addressed by increasing auditing activities (Jannelli, 2012) (Table 2.1).

Table 2.1 The complexity in the use and in the implementation of accrual accounting

The complexity of accrual accounting implementation		
Source	Research approach	Findings
Lapsley (2012)	EX POST ANALYSIS: The effects of implementation	The mutation of accrual accounting
Christiaens and Van Peteghem (2007)		Accrual accounting no compliant
Arnaboldi and Lapsley (2009)		The ambiguity of accrual accounting
Nesbakk and Mellemvk (2011)		The discretion in the accrual accounting implementation in the construction of materiality
Connolly and Hyndman (2006)		The non-neutrality of accrual accounting
Christensen and Parker (2010)		The phantom image of accrual accounting

Looking at the table, studies of accrual accounting implementation in many countries have found similar difficulties in detecting effective systems in use. Looking at the "findings column", what is clear from this study is that the outcome of these reforms remains uncertain. However, all of this prior research comes from ex post studies. In other words, most of these studies are focused on systems which were already in existence. The main objective of these studies has been to look at the effects of implementation.

This research differs from the existing literature by undertaking an analysis which is both *ex ante and processual* (Pettigrew, 1997). This perspective has been deployed in studies of *accounting in action* (Briers & Chua, 2001; Miller & O'Leary, 1990; Robson, 1992; Preston et al., 1992; Christensen & Skaerbaek, 2010; Joannidès & Berland, 2013).

2.4 Prior Studies in Accounting in Action

In the literature, other theories have been used in accounting change research. The Contingency approach (Otley, 1980) aims to identify the direct relationship between accounting and the environment. Some models have been developed according to this theoretical approach. There was a wide range of use of the contingency approach in the private sector (Innes & Mitchell, 1990; Kasurinen, 2002) and in the public sector where the pioneer was Lüder. Over the years, his model has been enriched by the contributions of other scholars (Godfrey et al., 2001; Saleh & Pendlebury, 2006) and subsequently used to extend the examination to local levels of government (Mussari, 1995; Yamamoto, 1999) and universities (Upping & Oliver, 2011). The contingent variables explain the "why" and "how". The same measure in the field of accounting (sometimes accrual accounting) is implemented in a different way within organizations. However, this theory is not able to explain the changing nature of accounting systems. Equally, the agency theory (Evans & Patton, 1987) and the isomorphism theory (Powell & Di Maggio, 1983) have been widely utilized in accounting change analysis. But all these approaches were not able to explain the way in which the system in itself undergoes mutation and alteration. The *accounting in action* approach fills this gap.

Adopting the *accounting in action* perspective, the implementation of accrual accounting in the public sector can be conceived as a *dynamic and controversial process*. Numerous studies on accounting change have adopted the "accounting in action" approach, such as Miller (1991), Preston et al. (1992), Chua (1995), Briers and Chua (2001). In this research, adopting this approach means that accounting changes are analyzed using the theoretical framework by Latour of "Science in Action" (see Chap. 2).

Briers and Chua (2001) were among the first Actor-Network Theory (ANT) scholars to have taken issue with the implementation of private sector innovations, the activity-based costing, in the public context. The aim of this research was to illustrate how accounting changes occur, and more precisely how networks (local organizational action) influenced this process. Specifically, the authors analyzed the implementation of ABC and the role of *actor-network* and *boundary objects* in this accounting change. Specifically, the authors argue that the accounting change is not influenced by social factors but is molded by the hands of inventors. Change is also prompted by the action of an inter-organizational network and is ultimately a social accomplishment by many different *human* and *non-human* elements. The authors talk about boundary objects, "which are both plastic enough to adapt to local needs" (Briers & Chua, 2001, p. 241) and at the same time "robust enough to maintain a common identity across cites" (Briers & Chua, 2001, p. 241). This ideal boundary is "hard outside and in plastic inside", so it can be shaped to suit different requirements (Briers & Chua, 2001, p. 242). This is the reason why two companies may both adopt an activity-based costing, but the "machine" is different and as a consequence "they do different calculations" (Briers & Chua, 2001, p. 240).

Miller, in his 1991 paper, "Accounting innovation behind the enterprise: problematizing investment decisions and programming economic growth in the UK in the 1960" analyzed the usage of the Discounted Cash Flows (DFC) technique for investment decisions within firms. Adopting Latour's approach, the author argues that accounting innovation is related to the concept of *Programs, Translations,* and *Problematization.* These are typical terms from Latour, and the meaning is "offering new interpretations of particular problems and channeling people's thoughts in specific directions" (Miller, 1991). The author clearly shows the way in which particular calculative technologies (Discounted Cash Flows) can come into play in articulating programs. It clearly illustrated the failure in the translation of the idealized programs within which DCF showed the indirect effect of these kinds of "technologies".

Miller, in 1998, argues that innovation in accounting takes place not only at its *margins,* but also through a process *of problematization.* The image that Miller provides of accounting is similar to a "*bricolage*", an activity whose instruments are mostly unrehearsed and transposable to suit the materials and the purposes which are to serve. The transformation of accounting as a body of expertise takes place within and through a historically specific ensemble of relations formed between a complex of actors and agencies, arguments and ideals, calculative devices and mechanisms. It is such ensembles or assemblages that need to be addressed (Miller, 1998, p. 618).

In 1992, a paper by Preston called "Fabricating budget: a study of the production of management budgeting in the national service" explores the emergence of accounting and budgeting in a healthcare organization. Adopting the perspective of "*accounting in action*", the author investigates the translation of private sector instruments, such as budgeting and accounting into hospital management. The author claims that the purposes of accounting systems are not well defined in the documents associated with the management budgeting initiative. This is specifically true when it comes to the characteristics of implementation, purpose, and new possibilities for decision-making. As a consequence, it is fabricated in a fragile manner. The author expresses the notion of *fabrication*, as an attempt to examine the chains of reasoning and mechanisms of influence between structured forces in the determination of the direction of change and human agency in the determination of the pace of that change (Preston et al., 1992, p. 565). The notion of *fabrication* is articulated in three "images" and includes three different concepts, which are as follows:

1. *To Build*: The process of construction, the blueprint of the project, how a budgeting system can be designed and shaped in order to meet "specifications" (Preston et al., 1992, p. 565) or guidelines.
2. *Fragility*: Expresses the lack of resources during the implementation and the during the maintenance of the system. This weakness could result in a failure.
3. *Machinations*: Is using a rhetorical synonym (the political machinations) to tell convincing stories about the benefit of a budgeting system. It indicates the plan to sell the new system benefits and purpose to skeptics.

The term "Fabrication" was chosen by the author instead of "Production" or "Construction" or "Translation". The main motivation is because the term "fabrication" incorporates the other terms. The term "Production" is just focused on the building process and is not able to include fragility and machination. The term Construction was used by Miller in accounting studies. It indicated "the way in which accounting together with other practices serves to construct a particular field of visibility" (Miller & O' Leary, 1987, p. 239). Translation is a typical term by Latour's analysis of science in action, which is used to make sense of the transition (Latour, 1987, p. 108) and emphasizes just the machination dimension. In its paper, the author outlines the difficulties of developing a plan to sell the advantages and the usefulness of the budgeting implementation system. Among skeptics there was scarce will to overcome resistance to change. Moreover, the author describes the crucial role of both the *consultant* in the organization *and the social conditions* when it comes to successfully operating such a system.

A study by Christensen and Skaerbaek analyzes the influence of consultancy activities in public sector accounting reforms using actor-network theory. Specifically, it illustrates the *purification* of accounting innovation in the public sector through consultancy activities. "*Purification* is a process of transforming opinions or statement into hard facts" (Christensen & Skaerbaek, 2010, p. 527). In their paper, the authors compare the Danish and Australian public sectors and clearly describe how private consultants operate in this specific context, achieving the power to influence the implementation of accounting innovations (Christensen & Skaerbaek, 2010, p. 525).

A recent paper by Joannidès & Berland (2013), which adopts the accounting in action approach, outlines how accounting knowledge is produced. The authors follow the actors, both human and non-human (researchers, Ph.D., journals) in the construction of accounting knowledge. It states that accounting knowledge comes from a multiple-translation process (Table 2.2).

Thus, studies of the adoption of accrual accounting in the literature reveal complexities in the use and in the implementation of an accrual accounting system. These findings have intensified debates about the merits of accrual accounting in the public sector. This study extends this prior literature, by utilizing the framework of the creation of technologies (Latour, 1987; Preston et al., 1992). This research also extends the prior literature of *accounting in action* because it adopts a distinctive perspective. It is a study that examines how organizers shape an accrual accounting system from its initial stage of implementation, such as the emergence of new technologies. Moreover, this study extends prior literature about the *complexities* of

Table 2.2 Main studies of accounting in action

Accounting in action: main studies which addressed to Latourian approach		
Source	Research approach	Findings
Preston (1992)	ACCOUNTING IN ACTION Latourian approach	Management budgeting is fabricated in a fragile manner
Miller (1991)		The failure in the translation of discounted cash flow
Miller (1998)		Accounting is a "bricolage"
Briers and Chua (2001)		The implementation of activity-based costing is socially determined by the moulding of inventors
Christensen and Skaerbaek (2010)		The purification of accounting innovations in public sector by the consultancy activity
Joannides and Berland (2013)		Accounting knowledge comes from multiple translation processes

accrual accounting implementation and sheds fresh light on the nature of accrual accounting introduced by government because it adopts an *ex ante perspective*. This approach is critical of the assumption that accrual accounting is well defined by policy-makers and that the portability of commercial accounting to a government setting is a *neutral fact*.

The particular focus of this study is on the *emergence* of accrual accounting as a new technology. The major contribution of this research is its critical evaluation of the factors involved in the first phase of implementation of an accrual accounting system in which new forms of accounting are engineered and fabricated.

This research has not presented a general overview of a reform on public sector accounting in a country nor about the set of reforms undertaken in Europe, which are generally classified under the umbrella of New Public Management. Additionally, this study has not conducted a survey about the organizational conditions, the application, or the outcome of a reform. The objective of this study is not to reflect on operational conditions that facilitate or hinder the organizational change during its implementation. Conversely, the focus of this research will be on a single "practice": accrual accounting. Studies, including Lapsley (2012), Christiaens and Van Peteghem (2007), Arnaboldi and Lapsley (2009), Nesbakk and Mellemvik (2011), Connolly and Hyndman (2006), and Christensen and Parker (2010), show that this research is *critical* to the assumption that accrual accounting systems are considered politically neutral mechanisms for enhancing strategic decision-making and for improved efficiency in evaluating performance and service costs (Guthrie, 1998). However, this study is not based on implementation issues.

This study differs from the extant literature on accrual accounting, which has focused on the arguments "for and against accrual accounting", the use of the information produced by accrual accounting system, or the technical difficulties of implementation. This research will instead analyze a reform in public sector accounting that has often attracted scholars—the introduction of accrual accounting. However, the assumption of this study came from studies of accounting in action and addresses these matters by looking at the following (Fig. 2.1).

- The *reform* as a process of translation of an actor-network. The implementation of a reform policy by the government is not a linear process, but the result of the actions of those who contribute to this "shift". The *translation* (Callon, 1986) of a reform implies a transformation in the object that is being transferred. The theoretical framework of the sociology of translation is born inside of technoscience theories drawn from Latour. This issue will be developed in Chap. 2.
- *Accounting* is seen as a set of practices, referred to as "calculative practices" (Miller, 2001), which are the result of a network of actions. Additionally, *accounting* is considered to be a "rhetoric machine" (Quattrone, 2009) as a conversation in which the various participants try to convince others of the superiority of a principle. Friar Luca Pacioli in 1494 published a treaty where is described the method of bookkeeping that Venetian merchants used during the Italian Renaissance "*Summa de arithmetica, geometria, proportioni e proportionalità*". The author approached accounting as a technology of remote control of capital, which operates with a coded language, double entry. Accounting was the rhetoric of numbers to construct reality and the way for traders of the time had of checking their capital. Some authors have defined accounting as the *art of memory*, but it is not just a neutral technique limited to reproducing the past. Accounting is defined as the construction in the present through technique, practices, and artifacts (Hines, 1988; Quattrone, 2009).
- *Government* is considered a set of emerging practices. The objective is to understand in what way the instrument (accrual accounting) has been translated and rewritten.

The research question beyond this study is: *What is accrual accounting for government?* In order to reply to this question, this study adopted an *ex ante perspective* instead of an ex post perspective. It follows the process of construction of an accrual

Fig. 2.1 Research's assumptions

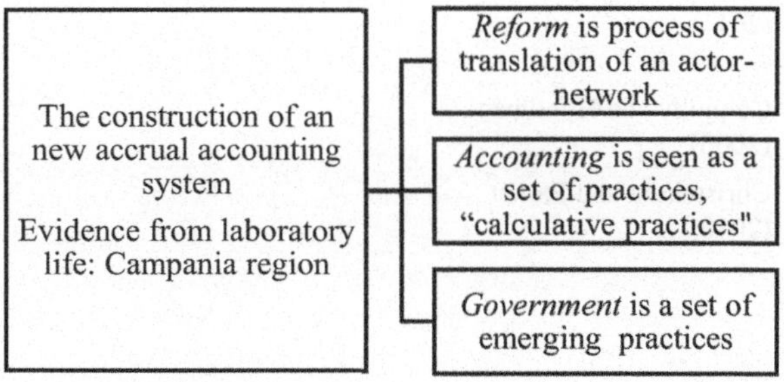

accounting system over a period of 2 years. It tracks the system from the time the policy was initiated, and implementation was explained to administrators in an official announcement, through its first stage of development. In other words, the objective of this study is to extend our knowledge of the process by which an accrual accounting system is devised and implemented in its initial stage.

The use of the expression "the *construction* of an accrual accounting system" instead of "the *implementation* of an accrual accounting system" or "the *diffusion* of an accrual accounting system" distinguishes this study from extant research and helps it to stand apart from the interpretative models that produced this research (Gherardi & Lippi, 2000). The studies, which adopted the term "*implementation*", have offered their greater contribution to the explanations of the gap between reform concepts and reform outcome (Steccolini, 2009) as well as the structural weaknesses of the reform projects and the difficulties of implementation (Lapsley, 1999; Lapsley & Pallot, 2000). Equally, the expression "*diffusion*" leads us to consider aspects related to complexity of accounting change in governments' organizational routine (TerBogt & Van Helden, 2000; Burns & Scapens, 2000; Caccia & Steccolini, 2006).

The scientific basis of the following research is to extend the trend of processual studies (Bruno & Lapsley, 2018) that shed light on the nature of accrual accounting in a special way revealing the myth of accrual accounting as self-evident (Lapsley et al., 2009). Adopting this distinctive perspective, accrual accounting as a technology and policy as a blueprint, we will entry in the black box, making an ex ante study, entering into a laboratory where experiments are taking place. Thus, once we clarify where this study is located in the literature, it is necessary to explicate the theoretical background for the study, the Latour's studies of *science in action* (Table 2.3).

Table 2.3 Main contribution to the literature

Source	Research approach	Findings
The complexity of accrual accounting implementation		
Lapsley (2012)	EX-POST ANALYSIS: The effects of implementation	The mutation of accrual accounting
Christiaens and Van Peteghem (2007)		Accrual accounting no compliant
Arnaboldi and Lapsley (2009)		The ambiguity of accrual accounting
Nesbakk and Mellemvk (2011)		The discretion in the accrual accounting implementation in the construction of materiality
Connolly and Hyndman (2006)		The non-neutrality of accrual accounting
Christensen and Parker (2010)		The phantom image of accrual accounting

(continued)

Table 2.3 (continued)

Source	Research approach	Findings
Accounting in action: main studies which addressed to Latourian approach		
Preston (1992)	ACCOUNTING IN ACTION Latourian approach	Management budgeting is fabricated in a fragile manner
Miller (1991)		The failure in the translation of discounted cash flow
Miller (1998)		Accounting is a "bricolage"
Briers and Chua (2001)		The implementation of activity based costing is socially determinated by the moulding of inventors
Christensen and Skaerbaek (2010)		The purification of accounting innovations in public sector by the consultancy activity
Joannides and Berland (2013)		Accounting knowledge come from multiple translation process
This research	EX-ANTE ANALYSIS: Latourian approach	Accrual accounting for government is not a well-defined technology, it is a fabrication, a machination

Chapter 3
Science in Action by Latour

Abstract This research is largely informed by studies on the social construction of science, whose most including the eminent scholar in this area, Latour (1979, 2013). Indeed, there are a number of social studies among science and technology topics that focus on the creation of scientific facts and examine how the scientist interacts to produce accepted technologies: the "social construction of technology" (SCOT).

The SCOT studies show "the constructivist character of science" (Latour, 1999, p. 115)[1]. SCOT studies have been developed using many approaches (Paul Verbeek & Vermaas, 2009). First, they look at technological artifacts as outcomes of the process of social interaction between designers and relevant social groups (Bijker, 1995). They also look at the interaction between both humans and a variety of non-humans, well known as actor-network theory (Latour, 1993). The SCOT has also been studied as a script for a theater play or a movie (Akrich, 1992) or on a more political level (Winner, 1986).

This is a different level of analysis. It represents a departure from the focus on *technologies* per se to *the social determinants of technologies*. In this study, this perspective is adopted to shift from accrual accounting as self-evident (Lapsley et al., 2009) to its construction through government policies (Bruno & Lapsley 2018). This study falls within extended research that looked at accounting as a technology (Preston et al., 1992; Miller, 2001). Specifically, the aim of this research is to extend our knowledge related to how accrual accounting systems are devised by policy-makers and implemented into the government structure, adopting a distinct view: *the construction of a new technology.*

---

[1]Andy Lock and Tom Strong trace philosopher of social construction back to the work of the eighteenth-century Italian political philosopher, rhetorician, historian, and jurist, Giambattista Vico. The criterion for truth would later shape the history of civilization in Vico's opus, the Scienza Nuova (The New Science, *La ScienzaNuova* 1725), because he would argue that civil life—like mathematics—is wholly constructed. Vico accepted a tutoring position in Vatolla (a little village near to Perdifumo), south of Salerno, which would last for 9 years. In 1699, he became a chairmanof rhetoric at the University of Naples. Source: *Wikipedia.*

A. Bruno, *New Public Management (NPM) and the Introduction of an Accrual Accounting System*, SpringerBriefs in Accounting,
https://doi.org/10.1007/978-3-030-57386-7_3

In these studies, the conceptual framework adopted by government is based on Latour's work *Science in action.* This study aims to understand the nature of technology (of accrual accounting) by examining the process involved in its *fabrication* (Preston et al., 1992). This research is not focused on the pre-constitutive roles of accrual accounting, but rather is concentrated on the process by which new designs, related to language, interpretations, and machinations, emerge through the fabrication of an accounting system. Studies related to the process of fabricating accounting focus on the creation of particular accounting technologies, looking at how systems are shaped for implementation in the organization (Preston et al., 1992). This study of the accrual accounting fabrication process is located in this field.

Thus, this research advocates an approach to accrual accounting that is based on "science studies". "Science studies" include a collection of humanities and social-science specialties that examine the contexts and the contents of science and technology. Why and how should we take a science-study approach to accrual accounting? One basis for doing so is to analyze controversies and to try and investigate technologies in the making, rather than looking at those that are already established. In other words, *opening the black box* (Latour, 1987, p. 4). The process of construction, and what is at stake during those processes, is the core of the investigation in a science-study approach, rather than a focus on consensual knowledge or established technologies. In this spirit, the introduction of accrual accounting in central government is examined with the aim of looking at this aspect of accrual accounting when the inner workings are still visible and before the technology is fixed, known and taken for granted (Preston et al., 1992). The research in science studies begins before the government bodies developing the accrual accounting processes are able to resolve construction controversies. Our research objective is to examine how technologies are fabricated.

In conclusion, there is a body of literature that focuses on the creation of scientific facts and technologies (SCOT). These studies offer an analysis of "what technologists and scientists do, and how they interact with each other and others to produce what will be accepted as a technology" (Preston et al., 1992, p. 563). The pioneer in this field is Latour; he "suggests that in order to better understand the nature of a technology we should examine the processes involved in its fabrication", thus "scientific facts and technical artifacts are not viewed as being part of a pre-existing natural order" but "the result of a process of fabrication" (Preston et al., 1992, p. 563). Latour's theory will be explained in this section.

3.1 Bruno Latour, the Anthropologist of Science

Bruno Latour worked for many years as a sociologist at the *Ecole des Mines* in high school for Engineers. Nowadays, he is a professor to *Sciences Po* a *Centre of political Science* in Paris. He is recognized as a philosopher of science, because he has offered an innovative perspective on the sociology of science. Latour has developed studies on the *creation of science and technology,* borrowing the methods of English historians and sociologists of science at the Edinburgh school (Latour & Woolgar, 1979; Latour, 1987, 1988).

During the 1980s, social constructionism theory (SCOT studies) emerged and continued to develop during the 1990s. Latour's studies draw on the theoretical approach of *Social construction* by Michel Foucault. In his studies, Latour uses a new approach to study *social objects in the making* following the actors and artifacts, including documents and the activity of experts and non-experts. The scientific facts are constructed by processes where human and non-human interests (technology) are mixed, and after negotiations have resolved. In 10 years, the author published texts, which take a view based on anthropological science, and whose purpose is to explain, what is a scientific fact. "*Laboratory Life*", "*Science in Action*", and *Pandora's Hope* are the books that contain a rethinking of the theoretical concepts of science, technology, and action. *Laboratory life* was the product of 2 years of participant observation in an American laboratory designed to collect fieldwork of everyday laboratory behavior. The material collected shows that laboratory practices are not well organized and are without any logical progression or coherence. His findings are a disordered array of observations and scientist struggles to produce order. A laboratory is the place where social-political and technical aspects cannot be artificially separated in the process of pursuing science (Latour & Woolgar, 1986). The incontestable scientific facts are the result of long and laborious procedures that are messy and confusing (Luckhurst, 2006, p. 5). According to Latour, laboratory is a sort of "configuration of machine" (Latour & Woolgar, 1986, p. 65) and not merely a place that promotes social construction of science.

In the book *Science in Action,* Latour again demonstrates that science is socially produced and the black box represents a statement of fixed and uncontested scientific facts, without any controversy. Thus, it is necessary to open the black box to investigate the controversy. In the book *Pandora's hope,* Latour offers more elements about science in the making. He demonstrates how scientific practice, laboratory experiments, and fact "were clearly fabricated" (Latour, 1999, p. 15).

Latour's name is connected with the Actor-Network Theory (ANT), which he developed with his colleagues Michel Callon and John Law. It mainly focuses on the process by which diverse actors and institutions weave themselves together to create a *convergent network.* A network is the place where debates are organized and conducted. In other words, it looks at the relationship between the event, the objects, and related activities (Callon, 1986).

Furthermore, Latour has moved through philosophical and sociological studies to provide a new vision of nature, defined as the product, and not the cause of, scientific practices (Latour, 1999), law, religion, art and academic critique. Additionally, Latour develops policy studies, inspired by the theories of Machiavelli, which examine Italian political debates dating back to the sixteenth century in Italy. In this study, Latour reports thoughts he developed as "anthropologist of science" (Latour, 2011, p. 26). *Aramis,* for example, is a case study not located in a laboratory, but in a more social-political environment. Aramis, an automated rail system, was never adopted in Paris, despite its obvious technical superiority. The failure was due to lack of "translation". Latour used numerous citations from the novel Frankenstein by Mary Shelley when describing this failure, and indeed the image of Frankenstein brings to mind this techno-scientific project, composed of numerous different elements (Latour, 1996).

3.2 Opening Pandora's "Black Box"

Pandora's Box is an artifact in Greek mythology, taken from the myth of Pandora's creation in Hesiod's Works and Days. The "black box" was actually a large jar given to Pandora which contained all the evils of the world. Today, the phrase "to open Pandora's box" means to perform an action that may seem small or innocent but that turns out to have severe and far-reaching consequences.[2]

Black Box is the common name used to identify the electronic recording of data installed in an aircraft with the aim to facilitate investigations after an accident. Where should a study on science and technology begin? The innovative response of Latour can be summarized as follows: You might be thinking of traveling back and forth in space and time through flashbacks, opening *Pandora's black box*! (Latour, 1987). What does Latour's expression "opening a black box" mean? There are many *nuances* behind this word. A black box transforms given inputs into predictable outputs but the process that produces them is ignored; in other words, before a crash (or without a crash) contents of black box cannot be seen. Thus, "*Opening Black Box*" is used to explain the difference between two completely opposite perspectives: science already made and science in the making, the product and the production, *facere* and *factum*, to make and to do Latour and Woolgar (1979, p. 174). For these characteristics, this theory seems to be powerful for this ex ante research.

To explain the voyage through time and space, Latour illustrates three scenes representing three laboratories that have made scientific and technological discoveries.

1. In Paris in 1985, John Whittaker, a computer technician, was instructed by the Pasteur Institute in Paris, to create computer programs to make a three-dimensional representation of DNA strands. One day he turned on his computer, an *Eclipse MV/8000* and he was able to see the image of a DNA double helix in three dimensions.
2. In Cambridge in 1951, Jim Watson and Francis Crick presented the double-helix model. In the journal Nature, this model was established as the first accurate model of *DNA* structure.
3. In Massachusetts in 1980, Tom West developed a prototype for a new computer, the *Eclipse MV/8000.*

In Paris in 1985, John Whittaker got the images of the DNA on his computer, the Eclipse MV/8000. The key point is that the computer, a technological product,

[2]From Wikipedia. A definition is contained in the Glossary in the appendix.

and the *DNA, a* scientific product, are two "*black boxes*". Indeed, John ignores the *controversies* of the laboratory that have marked the stories of DNA's creation and Eclipse's creation as well. John does not know the stories and controversies related to the Eclipse's production. The company, based in Massachusetts (the Data General), was not willing to fund the computer prototype created by Tom West. However, this prototype had aroused interest in the marketing area, because the rival company (the Dec) would have placed a similar model on the market. It was actually a marketing manager that pushed for production. Similarly, John ignores the controversies that went on in the Cambridge laboratory related to the DNA studies. There, Sir Lawrence Bragg had ordered two scientists Jim Watson and Francis Crick to not spend time studying DNA. That's why John's perspective is made from science. He should have performed a flashback to understand these details. In other words, John would have had to open the *black boxes.*

Opening the black boxes means questioning the facts, returning to the uncertainties in the disputes among working groups and looking beyond ready-to-use science. In this voyage, it is necessary to investigate past controversies and try to understand how scientists and engineers are busy to dissolve it according to Latour; to do this, it is necessary to set aside any bias related to knowledge. The conceptual framework adopted is an entry into science and technology through the back door, by looking at the ingredients in the development of scientific knowledge, opening *the black box* (Latour, 1987, p. 4). Latour chose Janus as representation of science. Indeed, science has two faces, one that knows and another one that does not know. It is important to understand the one who does not know (Fig. 3.1).

Janus, according to ancient and myth, is the god of beginnings and transitions and consequently of gates, doors, passages, endings, and time. He is usually depicted as having two faces, since he looks to the future and to the past. The Romans named the month of January (Ianuarius) in his honor. Thus, to perform a voyage in science, it is necessary to set aside any bias related to knowledge that already exists and understand the perspective of those who still in the process, who did not yet have the answers, the science in the making.

There is a scarcity of information about the *production of the machines* and about the *production of scientific discoveries.* Products of science and products of technology are black boxes for us, because there are few people who enter to investigate.

Fig. 3.1 Janus Bifront, the opposite perspectives

What happens in the laboratory? Indeed, few researchers have investigated the cauldron that is *science in action*. To understand the nature of technology, it is necessary to study science in action and not science that is already made.

In Latour's theory, he defines black boxes *artifacts*,[3] underlying social processes that lead to its construction. Indeed, black boxes have an "undisputed role" in the context and practice in which they are used. The meanings and uses are, however, often taken for granted. Thus, each artifact hides its social process and its creator. Black boxes are the result of the interaction of many human and non-human actors as well as technical components, meanings, actions, and roles. Understanding their nature disrupts their finiteness and opens the black box, revealing their character.

A further element that characterizes the black boxes is that these are made durable, so they can travel through time and space, and remain intact during accidents. Thus, we have a series of disordered elements (inputs) that at some point become cohesive and operate as if they were one organized entity. It becomes a black box when a set of elements acts as one. Opening the black boxes allows one to go back to the time of disorder, when controversies are still available, before the facts are stabilized. Indeed, "when such cohesion is obtained we at least have a black box" (Latour, 1987, p. 131). This kind of process that should lead to cohesion follows the *building fact* or *artifact* process (Latour, 1987, p. 207). However, during this social process, it is possible for facts to mutate. For example, the invention of the bicycle was not an isolated event but a social process that lasted 19 years from 1879 until 1898 (Gherardi & Lippi, 2000).

Considering accrual accounting to be a black box is not just a linguistic artifice to surprise the reader, rather it is designed to connote its identity. In this sense, accrual accounting and other artifacts, such as a nuclear missile, television, or a bicycle, once built and entered fully into everyday use, become black boxes. Adopting an accounting in action research approach is equivalent to arriving before the black box is sealed and examining the fabrication of the accounting systems.

3.3 The Construction of Technologies: Starting from a Blueprint

This type of research sees construction as a process whereby something is being built, step by step until the final result is reached. It follows a logical scientific process, i.e., a blueprint. A blueprint is defined as a detailed plan of action. It is a technical text that forms the base for implementing new technology. When we get closer to ultimate scientific fact, whether a machine or technology, we enter into the heart of the controversies since the earliest stages of blueprints. "The scientific text is different

[3]An **artifact** or **artefact** (from Latin phrase *arte factum*, from *ars* skill + *facere* to make) is "something made or given shape by man, such as a tool or a work of art, esp an object of archaeological interest". "Artifact" is the only spelling in North American English, but other varieties of English also accept "artefact". Source: Wikipedia.

from all other forms of narrative (Latour, 1999, p. 56)". According to Latour's theory, when a technology is created, there is uncertainty about the effectiveness and the quality of the implementation process. For this reason, "technical texts should be constructed to withstand the assaults of an expected hostile environment" (Latour, 1987, p. 46). This thought could be synthesized in a sentence: "To read the sentences of the policy document without imagining the reader's objection is like watching only one player's strokes in a tennis final" (Latour, 1987, p. 46).

Latour has outlined the rules of methods of study the fabrication of scientific facts and technical artifacts. These rules are a guide to make the journey in technoscience (Latour, 1987, p. 59).

The first rule is the easiest and one that has generic value. It can be synthesized as follows:

1. *"The fate of facts and machine is in the hands of later users"* (Latour, 1987, p. 59). *Thus, our task is to Entry through the back door by analyzing not the product but the process of construction, before the boxes are closed and become black.*
   The second rule is more complex and requires more attention. It can be specified as follows:
2. *"By itself a given sentence is neither a fact nor a fiction; it is made so by others, later on"* (Latour, 1987, p. 25). Individuals are recipients who are able to turn a fact into *more of a fact* if it is inserted in a closed and strong premise, or *less of a fact* if it leads to uncertain objectives. In this case, our task is to analyze all the transformations that a statement undergoes instead of just looking at its intrinsic value (Latour, 1987, p. 57).

To define if a fact is *more of a fact*or, *less of a fact* is necessary in order to conduct an analysis of controversies at the earlier stage of construction of facts (when the box is still opened). The result depends on the type of *modalities (positive or negative)* that scientist, engineers, and politicians offer to push a statement in the direction of fact or fiction. *Modalities* are sentences that could be

- *negative* if we have skeptical recipients who deny an assertion;
- *positive* if there are recipients who confirm it.

Thus, the controversy becomes complex. Each replication increases the debate. The positive modalities lead us to the mountain, while the negative modalities lead us to the valley (see Fig. 3.3). Latour says that "the difference is as great as going up or down a river" (Latour, 1987, p. 25) (Fig. 3.2).

We have already said that the construction of the facts is a collective process. The third rule is that to convince other people (rhetoric), you have to ask friends for help.

3. *The number of external friends the text comes with is a good indication of its strength…* (Latour, 1987, p. 33).

To convince others, the information must appeal to allies, people of authority, who provide the strongest and most influential arguments. We use to do it when we insert citations of other authors in a text, or when we ask for assistance from people

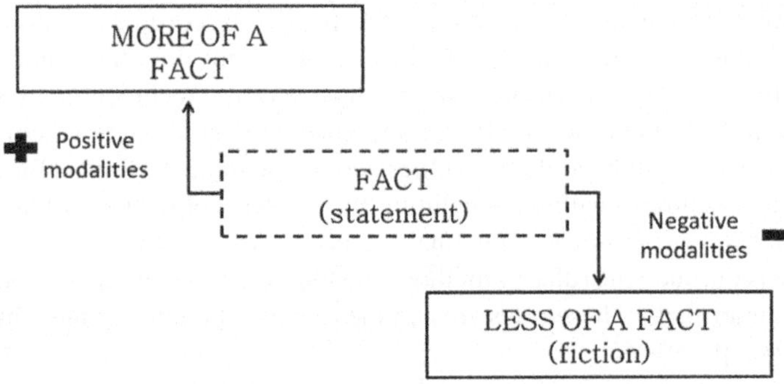

Fig. 3.2 The construction of fact

titled as professionals, academics, or consultants. Thus, an assertion is eroded or bolstered by the recipients. A fact is not a final product, but an artifact. Latour speaks of the malleability of artifacts (artifacts), because many hands are involved in their construction (see the definition page 8).

To explain this concept, Latour shows an example, using three assertions from the scientific field, which is reported here (Latour, 1987, p. 23):

(a) The primary structure of Growth Hormone Releasing Hormone (GHRH) is Val-His-Leu-Ser-Ala-Glu-Glu_lys_Gly-Ala.
(b) Now that Dr. Schally has discovered [the primary structure of GHRH], it is possible to start clinical studies in the hospital to treat certain cases of dwarfism, since GHRH should trigger the Growth Hormone that these individuals lack.
(c) Dr. A. Schally has claimed for several years in his New Orleans laboratory that [the structure of GHRH was Val-His-Leu-Ser-Ala-Glu-Glu-Lys-Glu-Ala]. However, by troubling coincidence, this structure is also that of hemoglobin, a common component of blood and a frequent contaminant of purified brain extract if handled by incompetent investigators.

Sentence (a) is as what we call a *fact* because it is not necessary to say more and the reader cannot go elsewhere for. It is an "indisputable assertion, a black box" (Latour & Woolgar, 1986, p. 23).

The sentence (b) builds on the initial assertion in sentence a) "will provide the firm ground to do something else (Latour & Woolgar, 1986, p. 23)", studies for dwarfism. Thus, the sentence became a black box, a fact taken for granted.

The sentence (c) contains the sentence (a) as well. However, this case is victim of a transformation because the reader is "led back into Dr. Schally's laboratory". This sentence indicates that controversies are still open.

"According to which direction we go, the original sentence a) will change status: it will be either a black box or a fierce controversy" (Latour, 1987, p. 24).

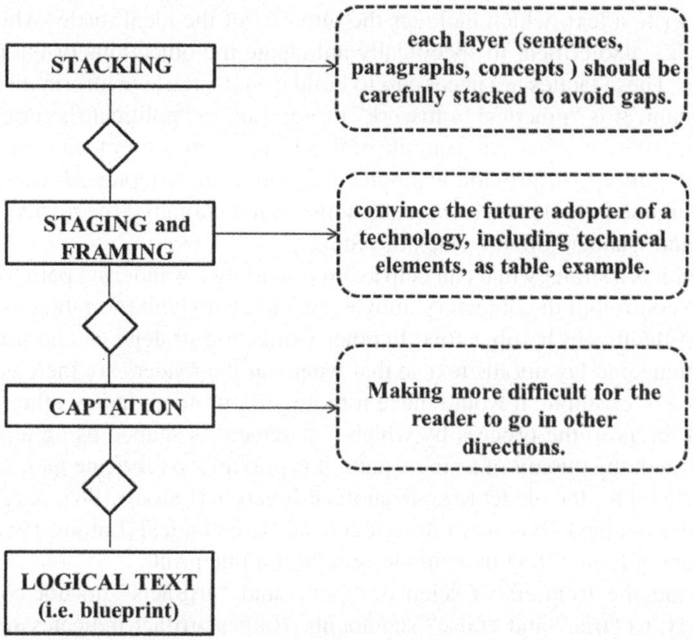

Fig. 3.3 Strategy for a logical text

Considering this rule, our analysis will allow us to understand which stage a statement was at the starting point of the controversy. We will be able to distinguish people who push for more of fact and people who push for less of fact. We can locate the statement, looking at Fig. 3.3.

3.4 The Strategy for Fortifying Text from Controversies

Latour describes a strategy for fortifying text from controversies, referring to papers. We will translate this issue to policy document and internal documents. The strategy for fortifying text is formed by specific steps designed to construct *logical texts*. The first one is *stacking*. Stacking is described as an activity similar to the building of a "stone hut". Each stone should go further than the one before it in the pursuit of a single path. This is a process by which each layer (sentences, paragraphs, concepts) should be carefully stacked to avoid gaps. In other words, we have a stack of layers and each one adds something to the preceding layer.

Although well stacked, the texts do not affect any change if casually read by any passing reader (Latour & Woolgar, 1986, p. 52). Latour refers to *staging* and *framing* as two strategies necessary to convince the future adopter of the value of a technology. In order to effectively convince these future adopters, Latour says that one must write a text, which includes the interests of the ideal reader who they are targeting. It's also critical to specifically anticipate the objections of the recipients in advance. These tactics are necessary to build easy-to-retrieve information into the text statement. It is "practical craftwork" as opposed to "political rhetoric" (Latour & Woolgar, 1986, p. 236). An example of this is the inclusion of technical elements, such as tabulations, to provide examples that guide the adopter. However, all the numbers amassed as relevant technical details are not enough if the reader is allowed to "stroll and wander" due to a lack of focus.

Captation is a strategy that can help avoid providing a wandering path for readers. It can also control all the objectors' moves. Indeed, with *captation* there is a "subtle control" of the moves by objectors. In other words, the strategy can be summarized in one sentence: to lay out the text so that wherever the readers are there is only one way to go. For example, it would make it more difficult to go in any other direction. *Captation* refers to the process by which a statement is shaped using a persuasive force. Through the pursuit of a single path, it is possible to fabricate *fact*, by making it more difficult for the reader to go in another direction (Latour, 1987, p. 52). "When such result is attained –It is very rare- a text is said to be logical (Latour, 1987, p. 58)". An example of *logical text* in technology field *is* a blueprint.

Following the frontiers of science, "facts" and "artifacts" do not correspond, respectively, to "true" and "false" statements. Rather artifact indicates *subjectivity* and fact, *objectivity* (Latour & Woolgar, 1986, p. 180). From a "constructionist" point of view, it is interesting to understand the way in which facts (objectivity) or artifacts (fiction, subjectivity) become incorporated into *technology* by policy documents and then, in our case, in an accrual accounting system. "The accuracy of the statement is not related to a state of affairs out there, but to the traceability of a series of transformations (Latour, 1999, p. 123)". This underlines the importance of observing the transformations statements undergo in policy documents and understanding them as either "fact or artifact" in the investigation. Latour describes the *collective controversy* game where antagonistic forces push a statement, from fact-like status toward artifact-like status. In other words, how does the black box, come into being?

3.5 The Construction and Fabrication of Fact: Laboratory Life

As in the social studies, in this research we use the words *construction* and *fabrication.* "Construct and fabricate are terms for technical activities. *Construction* implies a zero-sum game, with a fixed list of ingredients (Latour, 1999, p. 124)". However, "construction is in no way the mere recombination of already existing elements (Latour, 1999, p. 124)". *Fabrication* merely combines these elements in other ways. The implication is that if something is fabricated it is false. Likewise, if it is constructed it must also be "deconstructible" (Latour, 1999, p. 114). Understanding this definition and the difference between these key concepts is very important also

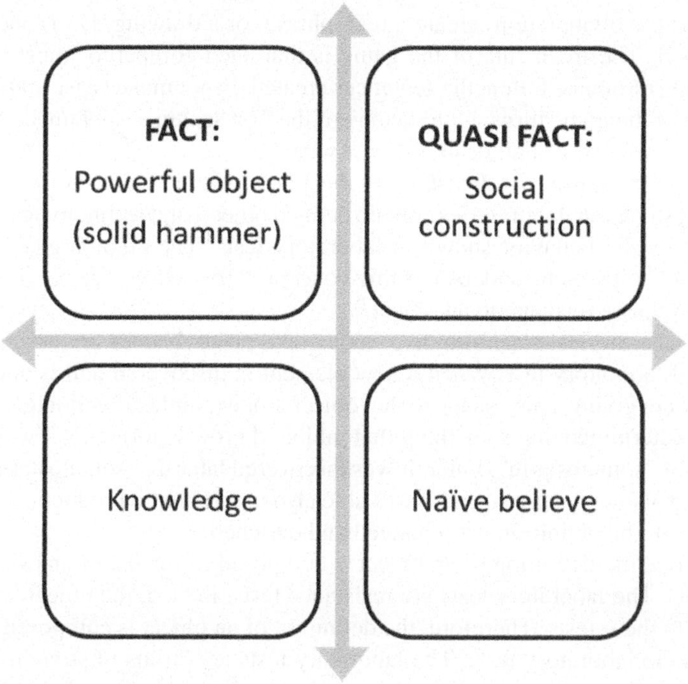

Fig. 3.4 Is it fabricated or is it real?

because these words "are the basic notions of *action* and *creation*" (Latour, 1999, p. 115). Indeed, "there is no other way to define an action but by asking what other actors are modified, transformed, perturbed or created by the character that is the focus of attention" (Latour, 1999, p. 122). "If we add to the facts their fabrication in the laboratory and if we add to the quasi fact their explicit and reflexive fabrication by their makers the main question is: are scientific facts real or are they constructed?" (Latour, 1999, p. 275). Latour explains this concept in Louis Pasteur's laboratory study, his empirical site at the Academy of Science (Fig. 3.4).

If we want to apply Latour's theory following *the construction of facts*, we have to go inside the *laboratories* (Latour, 1987, p. 63). Generally speaking, a laboratory[4] is a facility that provides controlled conditions in which scientific or technological research, experiments, and measurement may be performed. Thus, in an experiment, we will find experts, equipped with instruments to follow *the collective experiment* in a controlled environment (Bachelard, 2007). Latour, in his latest book *Cogitamus* (Latour, 2013), offers a definition of the *collective experiment* using the example of a French game called "*Cadavre exquis*". The goal of "Cadavre exquis" is to ask

[4]Laboratory is the place where scientific research and development is conducted and analyses performed, in contrast with the field or factory. Most laboratories are characterized by controlled uniformity of conditions (constant temperature, humidity, cleanliness). Source: https://www.britannica.com/EBchecked/topic/326,771/laboratory.

individuals to collaborate to create a text, phrase, or a drawing. Everyone involved has a pencil. The main rule of the game is that each competitor must ignore the contribution of others. Often, the sentences created do not make sense and are funny. The name of the game turns out to be one of the first sentences obtained, which was "The exquisite corpse shall drink the new wine[5]".

In a general sense, a *laboratory* is the place where scientists *discover facts.* According to Latour, laboratories contain defined objects and technologies. An object is *defined* by the behavior shown in laboratory tests. The etymology of the word "definition" helps us to understand this concept. "To Define" means to set limits, boundaries that give shape to an object.[6]

In the laboratories, scientific discoveries take place. Names are assigned to the findings of laboratory test. When a new element is discovered and is added to the object, we are giving a new shape to that object. For example, after numerous laboratory tests determined that something that inhibited growth hormone, it was assigned the name of "somatostatin". Later, it was discovered later that somatostatin had also been found also in pancreas, and it was able also to inhibit the production of insulin. At this point, the definition was changed and enriched.

Therefore, the definition of an object is composed of the list of answers to laboratory tests. The laboratory tests are resistance tests; indeed, the object is the set of reactions to these tests. Therefore, the definition of an object is composed of the list of answers to laboratory tests. The laboratory tests are "trials of strength" (Latour, 1987, p. 74). Generally, it is difficult to understand what goes on behind the walls of laboratories, because many elements are layered in other laboratories before and maybe elsewhere.

In the laboratory, scientists are routinely confronted by a "seething" mass of alternative interpretations (Latour & Woolgar, 1986, p.88). The solution adopted by scientists is the imposition of various procedures (Latour & Woolgar, 1986, p. 37). According to Latour, "an experiment is a story, is an event, is an action, is a text about a non-textual situation (Latour, 1999)". As a consequence, "no experiment can be studied only in the laboratory, only in the literature, or only in the debates among colleagues (Latour, 1999, p. 124)".

"A laboratory is constantly performing operations on statements: adding modalities, citing, enhancing, diminishing, borrowing, and proposing new combinations (Latour & Woolgar, 1986, p. 86)". The work of the laboratory can be understood in terms of the continual generation of a variety of documents, the *inscriptions* (Derrida, 1977). These are operations, more basic than writing, used to affect the transformation of the statements (Latour & Woolgar, 1986, p. 151). "A word replaces a thing while conserving a trait that defines it Latour (1999, p. 63)". "Member of our laboratory regularly noticed how their own assertions were rejected, borrowed, quoted, ignored, confirmed or dissolved by others" (Latour & Woolgar, 1986, p. 87). Scientists doing experiments isolated in a small circle who obtain results in the protected

---

[5]Exquisite corpse https://en.wikipedia.org/wiki/Exquisite_corpse.

[6]Define: to determine the boundary or extent of; (often passive) to delineate the form or outline of: the shape of the tree was clearly defined by the light behind it. Source: WordReference.com.

areas of the laboratory will have to move them from the laboratory to the real world. This process involves a series of tests, consultations, notes, and inscriptions. Thus, "the work of the laboratory can be understood in terms of the continual generation of a variety of documents, which are used to affect the transformation of statement types and so enhance or detract from their fact-like status (Latour & Woolgar, 1986, p. 151)". This framework is mobilized in this study. In this research, we are investigating what accrual accounting is for government and we need also to analyze what happened in the policy-making process: this is necessary because it helps us to clarify how accrual accounting system is constructed.

In *Laboratory life* (Latour & Woolgar, 1979), the author shows how scientific knowledge is produced in a laboratory and through a claim-making process. The logic of ANT emerges from having been initially developed in laboratory studies. However, in the ANT study (Callon, 1986), scientists in laboratories documented knowledge in the making, but it was more focused on human actors (scientists, patients) and non-human (resources, ideas).

In the process of constructing a new object, Latours started identifying different networks in which an object "had meaning (Latour & Woolgar, 1986, p. 124)". "This *process-oriented approach* is key to Latour's actor-network theory" (Levi & Valverde, 2008, p. 3).

According to ANT theory, the process of production is a success of *translation*. Indeed, there is a fourth rule:

4. "Society is made of groups which have interests; these group resist, accept or ignore both facts and machine (Latour, 1987, p. 141)".

This model lets us look at a "map of actors" involved in a policy reform process. It is concerned with all the processes by which diverse actors and institutions weave themselves together to create a *convergent network*. This *translating interest activity* is enacted through a series of translations (Callon, 1986), which explains the enrollment of people in these networks and in the construction of facts.

Latour borrows the concept of "*translation*" from Michel Serres, who uses it to describe a specific kind of mediation that simultaneously transmits and distorts signal. Up to this point, Latour creates the *sociology of translation*, which is now the core concept in a body of work that is also known as actor-network theory. In this research, translation aims to describe the challenges faced by fact-builders. Translation designates the ways in which such actors construe and otherwise related themselves to the interests of the other participants in the fact-building process so that they can recognize interests and goals (Latour, 2011).

The *translating interest activity* is moving through a series of translations, which explains how people enroll in networks. "During a controversy, operations of conviction mobilize a mixture of human and non-human agents (Latour, 1999, p. 99)". The translation process is composed of moments: problématization, intéressement, mobilization, and enrollment. For example, the structuring of a network occurs when a researcher determines that the network is worthy of academic interest; it is a *problematization.* A gap is identified and presented as a matter of concern for a community, and thus there is *interessement*. The community understands why this issue is worthy of investigation. Following there is *mobilization*, the engagement of other actors in the discussion. Actors within the controversies being studied develop contradictory arguments, *enrollment,* and points of view which lead them to propose different versions of "the social and natural words" (Callon, 1986). Thus, a fact is fabricated in the laboratory through a long and complex negotiation (Latour, 1999, p. 272).

In conclusion, we can say that "there is always more in the experiment than was put into it. Explaining the outcome of the experiment by using a list of stable factors and actors will therefore always show a deficit (Latour, 1999, p. 125)". In this deficit, there is fabrication, interpretation, and machination. There is a history of things, not only of science (Latour, 1999, p. 127). In this study, we will refer to the discursive process through which "things" that were previously different are made equivalent, thereby creating a system of homologies and convergences (Robson, 1992).

Below is a summary of the key ideas of this theory:

- To follow science in action and not science made looking at the construction of fact, i.e., opening black box.
- To desist from objectivity and subjectivity of the assertion (avoid from logical text) and follow the tortuous path that generated it, including controversies and "tribunals of reason (Latour, 1987, p. 179)".
- To enter into the place of controversies, the laboratory, analyzing comments made during the translation of interest.

The aim of this study is to analyze how accrual accounting is introduced, processed, manufactured, shaped, designed, and developed in a new context. It will reconstruct the institutional network, better defined as a *translator network* of the reform. The trial process is analyzed, and the forces at work affect (favoring and hindering) the birth of an accrual accounting system. The theoretical framework on which this research is located explains the origins of science. In this research, this theory is useful for an unusual and innovative reading of the creation of an accrual accounting system.

Chapter 4
The "Emergence Approach" from Direct Fieldwork Observations

Abstract This section contains the research method and the research context of this study. The research method explains how this analysis has been conducted; the research context describes the dissertation setting. This chapter does not list the research methods known in the literature; however, it will explain the methodology and data collection method chosen for this research, and the reasons for this choice included in the literature. In general, it is important to differentiate the methodology from the method. The methodology is the philosophical approach to the research. The method is the way in which the data are collected and analyzed. It is possible to use multiple methods of data collection using only one methodology; however, the method chosen should be closely linked to the research question. If this is the case, the important thing is to triangulate at the end. This is explorative research, an in-depth case study. It has adopted the constructionism research approach and a distinctive method for data collection, non-participant observation in video call conference. Even in the first part of the thesis, in which we do a content analysis of the policy, we maintain the constructivist approach. The research site of this research is Italy, specifically with a focus on the regional government in "Campania". The Italian case was particularly interesting since Italy, at the time of the data collection, was at a crucial point in the initial stage in its adoption of accrual accounting. Thus, the second part of this thesis describes the research context of this research. Specifically, it summarizes the Italian institutional setting and a brief excursus of reform in public sector accounting. Moreover, it presents specifics related to accrual accounting adoption in the intermediate level of government in the Campania region.

4.1 Research Approach

Generally, the choice of research strategy is related to the essence of the research questions and research objectives. It also relates to the chosen research approach and the researcher's ability. In this case, the research methodology was determined by its potential for realizing the research objectives. The main research objective of

A. Bruno, *New Public Management (NPM) and the Introduction of an Accrual Accounting System*, SpringerBriefs in Accounting,
https://doi.org/10.1007/978-3-030-57386-7_4

the study is to focus on the emergence of an accounting system to enrich our understanding of what accrual accounting means in practice for government. Studying these interactions, his will help us gain a deeper understanding. To do this study will employ qualitative strategies, functioning as an exploratory case study.

As explorative research, this study will adopt a constructionism approach. The reason for this is mainly related to the research question and research objective of this study. Indeed, in this study, the research question is, "What is accrual accounting for government?" To answer to this question is this study will explore how an accrual accounting system emerges among public entities. It adopts an ex ante perspective. The case study methodology has been chosen because "the case study is preferred when examining contemporary events but the relevant behaviors cannot be manipulated" (Yin, 2009, p. 12). The objective of this research is to expand theories. Indeed, a case study's analysis is generalizable to theoretical propositions (Yin, 2009). Specifically, in this study, an ethnographic research is conducted. The ethnography is a scientific method used in the social sciences to describe an approach to the study subject. This method of purely qualitative study relies on the "field" experience of researchers. Researchers must come into contact with the socio-cultural reality that it intends to describe. As Miller points out "Studies of the processes by which particular accounting practices emerge in specific contexts can be seen in a less favorable light than studies that draw upon a predictive model…." [however] "analyses of the conditions of emergence of such arguments, can help us to understand and explain why it is that a particular practice comes to appear problematic, and is eventually seen to be in need of modification or replacement" (Miller, 1998, p. 607).

Specifically, there are two opposing philosophical approaches underlying research methods in social sciences. The first is *positivism,* which essentially tends to test theory. The second is *constructionism,* which tends to explore the phenomena, discovering and building with the intention of adding something to the existing theories. According to the positivism approach, the social world exists "externally", and should be measured through objective methods. The constructionism approach states that a neutral exterior exists, but is socially constructed and given meaning by people. These "meanings" are varied and numerous, leading the researcher to look for the complexity of views. As a consequence, in the last case, the goal of the research is to rely as much as possible on participant's view of the situation being studied. Conversely, when using a positivism approach the researcher narrows these meanings into a few categories or ideas to measure. In most cases, the positive approach is accompanied by quantitative tests, for example, collecting data by using questionnaires. The goal is to confirm or disprove the hypothesis using statistical instruments. A constructionist approach uses a qualitative method as a case study, to investigate the phenomena. Thus, the first decision in any research project is to determine whether it is an explorative research or testing oriented.

4.2 Research Design

After establishing the research objective, the researcher should determine the unit of analysis and the research site, which is most appropriate for the project. The unit of analysis is the source of information. This could be an individual, a group, or an organizational document (Yin, 2009). The research site is the place where the study is conducted. This study was done on the accrual accounting implementation process in government. The unit of analysis, "the micro-world of the project" (Mosse, 2004, p. 642) is the regional government Campania region. This is one of the four regions involved in the trial. It is unique because it has never implemented an accrual accounting system in the past (Fig. 4.1).

In this study, it is possible to separate the analysis into two phases: a macro-sociological study and a micro-sociological study. The objective is to observe the difference between the logic of scientific practices (creation of technology) and the logic of non-scientific practices (fabrication practices) where interpretations are created and sustained within the laboratory. The design of the system only represents part of the construction process. The second part of this analysis looks at the emerging definitions of accrual accounting in video call conversations. Specifically, the first phase conducted a documentary analysis, followed by an in-site observation. Before analyzing how accrual accounting was shaped in the public sector, it is necessary to understand the meaning of accounting and to focus our attention on the analysis of two key elements behind a government process of reform. The first one is the policy documents by which the reform is mapped out. The second one is the network of institutional actors behind the text and any controversies key institutional players.

The second phase includes non-participant observation in an in-depth case study in the Campania region (Yin, 2009). The selection of the case study was based on the following factors. The first reason was the nature of the study unit of analysis in which theoretical factors were considered. Previous studies that have investigated accrual accounting practices in Italy's regional governments revealed several challenges (Borgonovi, 2005; Pezzani, 2008).

The second reason is that those responsible for the regional accounting trial, unlike, local government, are the only ones who participate in the tables directly and

Fig. 4.1 Micro- and macro-perspective

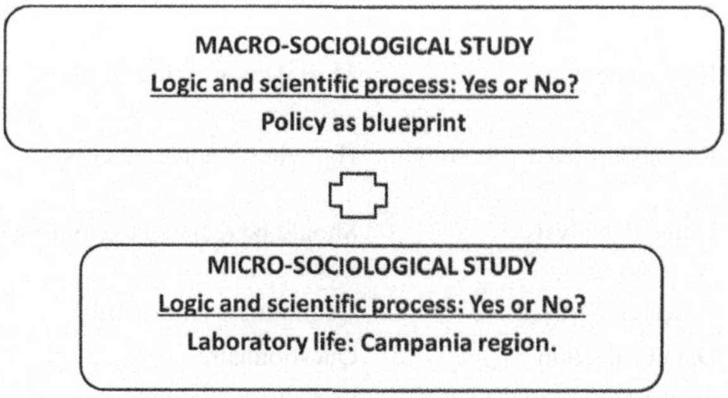

have the power to contaminate and change the reform. They represent human actors who are active in the network. They can deeply change the outcome.

There were four regions officially involved in the trial including Campania, Lazio, Basilicata, and Lombardia. There are two reasons why we chose to focus our study on the Campania region. First of all, it is the only region that has never implemented an accrual accounting system. In the other regions, a partial introduction of an analytical cost center was used in the past. Secondly, it has been obtained in-site observation data from the Campania region, which had the easiest access to reserved data.

4.3 Data Collection

Policy documents formally guide government reform. A blueprint specifies all the aspects and phases involved in the construction of technologies. A policy that includes established, technical, managerial social, and economic conditions reduces the possibility of weakness or hesitancy among adopters. However, unspecified conditions can also influence a system's evolution. Policy analysis follows this first guideline, adopting this framework (policy as a blueprint). The analysis of relevant policy documents allows researchers to capture the meaning of accrual accounting and enhances their understanding of how the reform process unfolds.

The data collected for the documentary analysis in phase one consisted of a variety of policy documents (see Table 4.1).

These documents included:

(a) *State documents* including laws and Decrees from Ministry of Economy and Finance; Decrees of the Prime Minister; Policy documents from the State General Accounting Department, the Supreme Audit Institution (Corte dei Conti), the Constitutional Court (Corte Costituzionale) Committee reports, such as Committee for the Chart of Accounts (Comitato per I prinicipi contabili), the Conference State-Regions (Conferenza Stato-Regioni).

Table 4.1 Research paradigm

	Positivism mainstream	Constructionism ethnographic
The observer	Must be independent	Is part of what is being observed
Explanations	Must demonstrate causality	Aim to increase general understanding of the situation
Research progress thorough	Hypotheses and deductions	Gathering rich data from which ideas are induced
Units of analysis	Should be reduced to simplest terms	May include the complexity of whole situations
Research Method	Quantitative (statistical)	Qualitative (case study)
Data Collection	Questionnaires	Observations
Generalizations throughout	Statistical probability	Theoretical abstraction

(b) *Regional documents* including regional laws, accounting rules, regional Committee Resolution. Other internal documents were also analyzed, including reports of the State-Regions Conference, in which the Ministry met representatives of the regions, the protagonists of the implementation, and reports and documents from Technical Committees setup for implementation.

In addition, the State General Accounting Department's (Ragioneria Generale dello Stato) website contains a very interesting section of FAQs (Frequently Asked Questions). Here, it is possible to read all the answers to frequently asked questions, including a common solution to any implementation problem. Specifically, these FAQs are related to

- references to the legislation, because according to the Art. 2 of Decree of 28th December 2011, the provisions related to the trial are applied "on an exclusive", replacing the accounting system previously in force;
- the critical issues and difficulties encountered in the accounting trial, for example, related to the ICT system.
- the requests for clarification related to the application of general and applied accounting principles. This was monitored by the publication of the updated principles[1]; among these are the accounting instructions and descriptions of particular situations related to the implementation of accrual accounting (Table 4.2).

These FAQs were continuously updated, and it was very simple to view them via a dropdown menu.[2]

The Ministry of Economy and Finance, to start the accounting trial, delegated responsibility to the General Accounting Office, specifically the "Arconet group" to manage the trial. Moreover, the Ministry has set up "working groups" (Working Group n. 1), which work under the Joint Technical Commission for the implementation of fiscal federalism. This group is dedicated to '"budget harmonization of regional and local authorities". A smaller subgroup works under the working group and meets every Tuesday.[3] This subgroup has the task of guiding and monitoring the progress of the activities carried out by institutions in the trial. The members of this subgroup are academics, like Professor Ricardo Mussari[4] who is an expert in public accounting, representatives of the Italian Banking Association (ABI), and representatives of Local Governments Associations (ANCI) and representatives of Accountants (ODEC).

---

[1]http://www.rgs.mef.gov.it/VERSIONE-I/e-GOVERNME1/ARCONET/PrincipiContabili/.

[2]http://www.rgs.mef.gov.it/VERSIONE-I/Faq/.

[3]http://www.mef.gov.it/ministero/commissioni/copaff/documenti/Riunioni_COPAFF.pdf.

[4]Riccardo Mussari is Full Professor of Accounting in the University of Siena; among other things, he was President of International Public Management Network for 2011, 2012, 2013; he is Chair of permanent study group on public financial management of EGPA (European Group); he is member of the international editorial board of Financial Accountability and Managements in Governments Public Services and Charities. http://www.provincia.siena.it/var/prov/storage/original/application/41c35047d24fec76d8521c171610dd56.pdf.

Table 4.2 Policy documents about the implementation of accrual accountings

Date	Policy	Actor	
5th May 2009	Law n. 42/2009: decrees about reforming of public sector	Parliament	National Policy
31st December 2009	Law n. 196/2009: Cash accounting	Parliament	
20th January 2010	Report about Law 196	State General Accounting Department	
03-Mar-11	Agreement stipulates about Law 42/2009	Prime Minister + Conference State-Regions	
7th April 2011	Law n. 39/2011 Modify the 196/2009	Parliament	
17th May 2011	Report about Law 42/2009	Supreme Audit Institution	
31st May 2011	Legislative Decree n. 91: Trial period, implementation	Ministry of Economy and Finance	
24th May 2011	Report about the implementation of the reform	Committee for fiscal federalism	
24th May 2011	Report about the implementation of Law 42/2009 (Act. N. 339)	Research Department of Senate of the Republic	
8th June 2011	Report about the reform	Committee for fiscal federalism	
23rd June 2011	Decree 118: Reform of accounting system implementation of accrual accounting	Ministry of Economy and Finance	
28th December 2011	Decree: First selection of governments involved in the trial	Prime Ministry	
21st September	Region ask to post-pone the trial	Conference State-Region	
29th December 2011	A Decree Post-pone the trial period for the implementation	Prime Minister	
18th April 2012	Report about National Reform Program of Public Finance Decision	Ministry of Economy and Finance	

(continued)

Table 4.2 (continued)

Date	Policy	Actor	
10th May 2012	Semestral Report about the implementation	Parliamentary Committee for fiscal federalism	
25th May 2012	Decree: Second selection of governments involved in the trial	Prime Ministry	
22nd January 2013	Semestral report about the implementation of accounting reform	Parliamentary Committee for fiscal federalism	
15th November 2011	Regional Decree: Preliminary activity is for the trial, teamwork	President of Campania Region	Regional Policy
29th December 2011	Regional Decree: the trial		
10th October 2012	Regional Decree: a KPMG partner was nominated as a consultant		
18th December 2012	Regional Decree: Individuation of Consultant for the implementation		
3rd March 2011	Text of Decree 118/2011, discussion and modification	Technical Committees + Conference State-Regions	Internal Documents
10th September 2012	Text of Decree 118/2011, discussion and modification Part III	Technical Committees – Conference State-Regions	
25th September 2012	Draft modifications on chart of accounts, budget, financial reporting	Ministry of economy and Finance + S.G.A.D.	
11th December 2012	Draft for Discussion: implementation in healthcare sector	Working group + KPMG	
21st December 2012	Text of Decree 118/2011, discussions and modifications	Working group+Ministry	
7th January 2013			
23rd January 2013			
30th January 2013			

Every week, the group Arconet selects FAQs from the website. These are the items on the agenda to be discussed in the meeting with the working group 1 and with those responsible for the accounting trials. These regional authorities also take part in the meetings organized on Tuesday. At these meetings, group members create a document which contains FAQs, and it is sent by email to each participant. Prior to these meetings being established, the regional representatives responsible for the accounting trial voluntarily agreed to organize a video conference call on Monday to these agenda items in advance. During these video conferences, call group members share experiences, doubts, and misgivings regarding the measures that are being implemented. Specifically, the analysis of a single FAQ on the agenda is done by looking into the internal situation. The main focus of the discussion is the agreement or disagreement with the resolution provided by the Arconet group. Sometimes, an alternative solution is proposed. All the ideas born of this discussion are written in a new report, which is presented the day after to the institutional meeting. Reports from both the video conference call and institutional meeting are collected and analyzed. These discussions also involved others aside from those responsible for the trial in each region, including employees from different sectors, for example, property, and heritage assets' representatives will attend if some points of the discussion are related to that field. Meetings may also include accountants and consultants (Table 4.3).

4.4 Research Context

Italy ranks ninth among the countries of the world when sorted by their gross domestic product (GDP). In recent years, Italy has started on an ambitious program of reform aimed at restoring the sustainability of public finances and to improve the country's long-term growth. Italian public debt is among the highest in the OECD countries and for the next two decades will exceed 100% of GDP. Indeed, with a public debt / GDP ratio close to 130%, Italy remains susceptible to "sudden changes in the mood of the financial markets". Low growth and persistent budget deficits are at the base of the stubbornly high level of public debt.

The high level of debt makes Italy particularly exposed, in the current economic and financial crisis where a vicious cycle is playing out in public finances, the financial sector and the real economy. Since the summer of 2011, financial markets have begun to seriously doubt the sustainability of Italian public debt, resulting in an increase in spreads on government bonds.

In the autumn of 2012, after a series of structural reforms, the interest rates for the Italian public debt were reduced. However, interest rates were still much higher than the German rates. This spread is due to the high level of public debt. Thus, national government has made it a priority to reduce public debt, promote growth, and improve competitiveness putting Italy on the path to healthy growth. A move to consolidate public finances also began in 2012 and is still ongoing. According to the OECD, the total public debt would stand at around 134% of GDP at the end of 2014. Its renewal will require about € 400 billion a year, over the next few years (OCSE, 2013).

Table 4.3 Meeting's data collected

The Meetings of the Sub Working Group n. 1 '"Budget harmonization of regional and local authorities" of the Joint Technical Commission for the implementation of fiscal federalism (COPAFF)

2013

January	February	March	April	May	June	July	August	September	October	November	December
08/01/2013	05/02/2013	05/03/2013	04/04/2013	07/05/2013	06/06/2013	02/07/2013			08/11/2013	05/11/2013	03/12/2013
15/01/2013	14/02/2013	12/03/2013	09/04/2013	09/05/2013	11/06/2013	09/07/2013			15/10/2013	12/11/2013	10/12/2013
22/01/2013	19/02/2013	14/03/2013	11/04/2013	14/05/2013	25/06/2013	16/07/2013		24/09/2013	22/10/2013	19/11/2013	17/12/2013
29/01/2013	26/02/2013	19/03/2013	16/04/2013	21/05/2013		23/07/2013			29/10/2013	26/11/2013	
31/01/2013	28/02/2013	26/03/2012	23/04/2013	28/05/2013							

The Video conference call

2013

January	February	March	April	May	June	July	August	September	October	November	December
		04/03/2013	03/04/2013	06/05/2013					07/10/2013	04/11/2013	02/12/2013
14/01/2013		11/03/2013							14/10/2013	11/11/2013	09/12/2013
21/01/2013	25/02/2013	25/03/2013				15/07/2013			21/10/2013	18/11/2013	16/12/2013
28/01/2013								23/09/2013	28/10/2013	25/11/2013	
			29/04/2013								

The Italian government is working to increase the ratio of public debt to GDP pointing to a budget in state general balance or a small surplus. However, a good public governance reform is important for economic growth. Thus, there have been important steps in the field of public administration and civil justice reforms to support economic development and the needs of civil society (OCSE, 2013) more effectively.

The national government has introduced reforms aimed at improving the performance of public administration with the aim of increasing accountability and encouraging a performance culture. In all levels of government, the focus on transparency still remains; however, it seems that governments have focused only on prescriptions that include sanctions and do not recognize the importance of transparency (CIVIT, 2012). On the contrary, the success of the reforms in the public sector mostly depends on the creation of a cultural change within the bureaucracy.

Moreover, the anti-corruption law (Law n. 94, 15 July 2009) provides the most effective tool to fight against corruption and organized crime. In Italy, the corruption in the public sector is more severe than in other OECD countries (OCSE, 2013). In 2012, the governors of two regions (Lazio and Lombardia) resigned following charges that they embezzled public funds. In 2013, 183 public entities were also suspended because of the control of criminal organizations. Currently, there are nine regions covered by these events (Sicilia, Calabria, Campania, Puglia, Basilicata, Lazio, Liguria, Piemonte, and Lombardia). The first in the blacklist is Campania (where even a Local Health Centre has been suspended "Azienda Sanitaria Locale Napoli n. 4"), followed by Calabria and Sicilia. The three regions the three largest criminal organizations operate include "Camorra, Cosa Nostra, 'Ndrangheta".[5]

These events are not new but have a long history. In 1990, a crisis emerged in the political system (bribesville) that deeply shocked the public and resulted in a series of political embarrassments, losses that ultimately transformed the parties. The normative framework in that period was characterized by the widespread need for transparency and accountability. The Legislative Decree n. 29/1993 outlined the division between political direction and administrative direction and the Parliament, through the Law n. 94/1997 (now Legislative Decree 165/2001). This prompted the Government to introduce economic analytic accounting by cost center. In 1997, the Government delegate (Law n. 94/1997, now Legislative Decree 165/2001) introduced economic analytic accounting by cost center in central government. The accrual budgeting and accounting system, although it involved both forecasted and actual determinations, limited its objectives to cost information. The main objective of the systems was the replacement of historical expenditure criteria. Two accounting documents that originated from this system are a national government accrual budget and a national government cost statement (Mussari et al., 2005). However, these administrative documents were issued as memorandums and were not subject to any type of parliamentary approval. This document also ignored one of the fundamental characteristics of accrual accounting, matching costs to financial year revenues (Anessi Pessina, 2007). The system was not integrated with commitment-based budgeting. In

[5]Source: http://it.wikipedia.org/wiki/Legge_contro_le_infiltrazioni_mafiose_negli_enti_locali.

fact, the information was to be obtained using cash accounting without an integrated budget accounting system. In the memorandum, information was created from an adjusting procedure and was used to transpose or at least to integrate the accounting data on an obligation basis (Mussari et al., 2005). It was a budgeting-accounting system, not one based on accrual criteria and it did not model an accrual accounting system. As a consequence, for many years, the accounting system in central government was related to these kinds of instruments. Therefore, in Italy, like in other countries, many reforms, which have aspects of New Public Management (NPM), have involved the government.

4.5 A Brief Overview of the Reforms in the Italian Public Sector

Italy is a democratic republic composed of the municipalities, provinces, and regions. Specifically, the State territory is subdivided into 1 state, 20 regions, 103 provinces, and 8100 municipalities. Regions and municipalities are autonomous authorities, which function with their own statutes and powers according to the principles established by the Constitution. During the last 20 years, there have been profound reforms, and many of these are still changing the institutional and administrative systems. These include the federal reform, which is not yet complete and possible abolition of the provinces. Italy is a civil-law country, with an institutional system typical of continental Europe. The government is characterized by the constitution and a separation of powers between the legislature and the executive branches of government. Public sector accounting is regulated by legislation. Central, regional, and local governments each apply the National law in terms of accounting budgeting and reporting system regulation. Therefore, the accounting standards are included in the law. However, regions have their own regulation (Legislative Decree 76/2000; Regional Laws, Regional regulation) and may use different public accounting systems. However, municipalities and provinces comply with a national statutory code that dictates accounting rules. The reforms of the regional finance system, which allowed for a large amount of autonomy both on the revenue and the costs management side, helped the gradual emergence of the Regions on the Italian institutional scene (Law n. 142 of 8th June 1990, Legislative Decree n. 504 of 30th December 1992 and Legislative Decree n. 56 of 18th February 2000).

The State General Accounting enriched the law providing information on practical arrangements to enable recognition of costs and to assist with budget preparation (Circular n. 32 of 1999, n. 23, 39 and 42 of 2000). These guidelines should encourage all public administrations to apply the new accounting system. Regions, in the short term, were using these tools. The region is a particular kind of public entity. It is responsible for the coordination and planning of public action within its territory. It does not directly provide public services but does provide funding to subordinate public bodies (municipalities) and to the actors operating within its territory (i.e., nonprofit organizations, universities, companies). The accounting system adopted by the regions had a mainly authoritative function, analyzing the financial management of the budget. This system also verified that management operations complied with regulatory standards and checked on those who administered revenues and expenses. In order to investigate the economic aspect of regional activity, the art 4 of the Decree 76/2000 introduced analytic accounting for cost centers.

The activities of the region are difficult to link with the economic analysis because of its intangibility, which prevents easy comparison of revenues and costs. A further complicating factor is that the system was not adopted by the majority of the regions as it was in the Campania region.

In 2000, the process of regionalization in Italy took a step forward. This progress, however, confirmed that it was necessary to adapt the institutional settlement and to reform the Constitution through a collaborative process between the various levels of government. It was also deemed necessary to delineate and coordinate the legislative powers (federalism reform). The federalism reform of 2001, enacted by Law n. 131 of 2003 on "Measures for the adaptation of the Republic of order 3 of the Constitutional Law of 18 October 2001", has been long and complex. The reform agenda mainly concentrated on the decentralization, which aimed at increasing the political, financial, and administrative autonomies of regional and local governments. The implementation of constitutional reforms involves the transfer of functions and resources, including financial resources, from the central government to the local government. Italy has achieved a significant level of decentralization in terms of expenditure responsibilities during these years. As such, more accounting information is expected to be produced by regional and local governments to inform political and administrative actors for decision-making. Through this evolution, regional politicians (regional councilors) along with administrative actors have gained mandates, which allow them to make budget decisions. The autonomy in accounting regulation has also been widely encouraged. The ability to self-determine the accounting structure allows regions to set up the accounting system in the manner that is best suited to their needs, albeit in compliance with established fundamental principles. However, this situation has led to the dishomogeneity between accounting systems, and therefore makes it increasingly difficult to compare information contained in the final documents.

Italy began an accounting reform in 2009, which is now underway. The Law 196/2009 reformed Italian public finances and accounting, adapting the legislative and regulatory framework to the needs of public financial and budgetary management. The Law addressed all the entities that make up the aggregate of general government as defined under the national accounting rules. The perimeter of Law 468/1978 (now abrogated) was extended. A consistent normative framework was laid down for all the entities that made up the general government. This was a harmonization reform in public sector accounting (Table 4.4).

Table 4.4 Previous reforms in Italy

Policy Document	Topic	Outcome
Law n. 94/1997	Parliament delegate Government to introduce an *economic analytic accounting by cost center*	Government carried this delegation into effect
Legislative Decree n. 279/1997 (now Legislative Decree 165/2001)	The introduction of the *economic analytic accounting by cost center* in order to show the economic profile of the expenditure	Explain the implementation in more than one step
Circular letter n.32 of 26 May 1999 and Circular letter n. 16/2002 of the Ministry of the Economy and Finance Ministerial Decree 25 March 2002	Cost information for qualifying the responsibility of management evaluating the consumption of resources The amendment of the *Single Chart of Accounts* the development of the computerized system the economic accounting portal	The system remains a budgeting-accounting system no based on accrual criteria. These administrative elaborations for cognitive purpose are not subject to any type of parliamentary
Legislative Decree n. 76/2000	Legislative Decree was a step forward in the process of implementation of accrual accounting	In spite of intentions, the system was not uniformly transposed
Law Constitutional Law n. 3/2001	Fiscal federalism reform. Reform of Title V of Constitution	The reverse of legislative powers between state and region. This aspect increased the complications related to the implementation of the reform because the boundary line between Region and State is not clearly defined. The Decree of Prime Minister 25 May 2012 reversed the regulation powers in public sector accounting regulations again, shifting them from the region to State
Law n. 131/2003 "La Loggia"	Delegate the Government to Reform the public sector accounting after fiscal federalism reform. Harmonization in budgeting and accounting system	Law, Legislative Decree from Government actually analyzed

4.6 The Italian Harmonization Reform

The process of harmonizing accounting systems in Italy is the answer to

- an internal necessity felt even at the constitutional level to enhance the comparability of public budgets and reporting systems in all level of government;
- an external necessity of a new institutional arrangement in the context of Italy's membership of the European Monetary Union (stability pact).

Harmonization is a process used to build comparable accounting summary documents for the whole public administration (Cañibano & Mora, 2000; Di Pietra, 2000). This process is complex because it requires the homogeneity of rules, models, glossaries, and procedures. Accounting is the process of identifying, measuring, and communicating economic information so that users can apply that information to make informed judgments and decisions. In the literature, it is possible to find *ex post* studies about harmonization (Van Der Tas et al., 1992). For example, one study defines the difference between *de jure* and *de facto* harmonization. *De jure,* harmonization is a process driven by a regulator, typically the legislature or another entity (such as the standard setter). *De facto* harmonization is spontaneous behavior accountants develop to achieve increasing levels of harmony (Di Pietra, 2000). International studies also detail the grade of harmony achieved after a harmonization reform. However, as highlighted by decades of past research, it is difficult to make a clear distinction between a de facto harmonization (spontaneous and more advisable) or de jure harmonization, which comes as a consequence of legal requirements. Thus, after decades of discussions, scholars have not achieved a common view on this topic. However, governments worldwide are making some efforts to adopt similar accounting systems.

The Legislative Decree n. 118 of 2011 established the general framework of accounting reform for regions, metropolitan cities, provinces, and municipalities, other institutions (entities instrumental in the regions and local authorities). The reform also concerns all the public entities, central/local/health agencies/company owned by minister of finance, which now apply very different accounting rules. A fundamental aspect of the current reform is the harmonization of the accounting systems and budget formats of general governmental bodies (Article 2). The harmonization of accounting systems and formats is provided, under the same standards and guidelines, for regional and local governments. An essential prerequisite for unified management of public finances is that the budget data for the various general government bodies are homogeneous, easily reconcilable, and promptly and easily accessible. Accounting systems and formats must also be reconcilable with those used for the European Union's excessive deficit procedure and consistent with the economic and functional classification set out in Community regulations (COFOG).

According to the reform on trial, the missions and programs budget of the Regions should be structured according to the State budget. This presupposes that the data are collected and presented in a shared format and follow the same accounting standards.

The statement on the expenditure is articulated as follows:

- Side missions: the main functions and strategic objectives pursued by the administrations (use financial resources, human, and material for this purpose);
- Programs (aggregates of activities used to achieve the objectives defined as part of tasks);
- Macro aggregates (articulation of programs, and economic category of expenditure), and on the side of income securities, types, and categories.

This structure ensures a more direct and transparent relationship with the purposes of expenditure and public policies. The unit vote for the approval of a balance sheet is formed, respectively, from the programs and types. The authorized budgets were formed on cash-based principles. The actual accounting system is based on a modified accrual and a modified cash basis. However, there is an innovative system of modified cash basis: payables and receivables are not recorded when arising but when coming to expiration (so-called reinforced modified cash basis).

In order to strengthen the budget planning function, the new configuration of the principle provides that both passive and active operations are recorded during the period when these are legally perfected and the accounting allocation of revenue and expenditure is made when the related liability or credit is due. Specifically, this new formulation is based on the distinction between three different moments in the life of the bonds. These include the birth, the chargeability (which is the phase in which the debt/credit becomes effective) and the extinction (Anselmi et al., 2012). This new principle also favors the modulation of debts according to the actual needs of financial institutions and prevents the determination of revenue future obligations and commitment (Ernst & Young, 2012; Pozzoli, 2012; Ricci, 2012a).

The enabling act allows organization to adopt uniform accounting rules and a common chart of accounting items.

The adoption of a common chart of accounts integrated should guarantee

- uniformity in the collection of operational events on the financial, economic, and property; preparation of consolidated financial statements with related agencies and instrumental organizations, companies, corporations, and other controlled entities;
- homogeneity with other accounting systems provided in the community.

Financial accounting is also flanked by a system of cost and asset accounting and a specially designed set of indicators for gauging results. This serves to reinforce the evaluation of government economic performance. The information system is completed by the introduction of consolidated accounts for general government bodies. These include firms that they own or control. For general government entities that are required to follow corporate (civil) accounting procedures, taxonomy must be devised to reclassify the accounts for reconciliation with the provisions governing the other entities.

Accrual accounting in the current reform is not the primary accounting system for the public entities. It will be only used for "cognitive purposes". The authorized budgets are still based on cash-based principles. Therefore, the cognitive purpose of accrual accounting is finalized:

- to recognize revenue and cost management to represent the "economic resources" acquired and used during an exercise;
- to participate in constructing account assets, which constitute a key performance indicator;
- to allow the preparation of consolidated financial statements for each public administration and to control their bodies and organizations instrumental, companies, societies, and other entities.

The Italian effort is a harmonization reform that is moving the government toward an accrual accounting system. It is the first time that a policy about public sector accounting has been implemented in a trial adopting a bottom-up process. The trial period began in 2011. It involves central government, local authorities, the health services, and public companies. It is scheduled to finish in 2014. The Decree of the Prime Minister (28th December 2011) defined the length of the trial period and said that it should involve central government, local government, and government agencies following geographical criteria, which includes 4 regions, 12 provinces, and 68 municipalities. In other words, experimental systems are now used for central and local subsectors. Definitive rules will be defined in 2014, based on the results of the ongoing experimentation (Meneguzzo et al., 2013). In 2014, the trial was extended to 300 entities. The full operation of this important reform will affect all the local authorities and their instrumental organizations beginning on January 1, 2015.

4.7 Unit of Analysis: Regional Government

In Italy, there are 20 regions. Fifteen regions have ordinary statutes and five have special statutes (Sardinia, Sicily, Trentino-Alto Adige/Südtirol, Aosta Valley, and Friuli-Venezia Giulia) granting them extended autonomy. These regions are autonomous because the government wanted to prevent their secession from Italy after the Second World War. A second goal was to take into account cultural differences and to protect linguistic minorities. Each region, except for the AostaValley (Valle D'Aosta), is divided into provinces and municipalities. Regions are autonomous entities with powers defined in the constitution.

Each region has an elected parliament, called the Regional Council (Consiglio Regionale) and a government called Regional Junta (Giunta Regionale), which is headed by the regional President. The nature of the Regions in Italy creates similar and different conditions among the Regions. Among the variations is the quality of infrastructure, such as healthcare, transport, and communication facilities. Differences can also be seen in terms of social status, education, and quality of life.

In the Italian Constitution of 1948, the regionalist idea takes shape as an intermediate solution between a federal state government and a centralized state model. Originally, the Italian administrative organization was similar to the French model. It exalted of municipal power, yet, the state possessed strong central power. Thus, the Constitution by art. 114 founds the Regions. Then in 1953, Law no. 60 of 10

February 1953 on *Establishment and operation of regional bodies* (Legge sulla Costituzione e sul funzionamento delle Regioni, called "LeggeScelba") lays the groundwork for the implementation of the regional government; however, it does not follow concrete actions in that direction. Only after 15 years under Law n. 108 of 17th February 1968 on Guidelines are the councils of the Regions elected (Legge sulle line guida per l'elezioni dei Consigli delle Regioni). Then Law no. 281 of 16 May 1970 on financial measures for the implementation of the Regions with ordinary statute (Misure finanziarie per l'attuazione delle Regioni a Statuto ordinario) begins the actual process of forming of the Regions. The Presidential Decree n. 616 of 24 July 1977 is a Consolidated Act as it recognizes the regional functions. Regions as autonomous bodies have statutory autonomy, which means the possibility of adopting its own regulation which relates to the discipline of the governance, internal organization and regulates all the activities not directly regulated by the Constitution.

All regions were governed under the same national financial and accounting regulation (Legislative Decree 76/2000 and Legislative Decree 170/2006). However, the autonomy in internal regulation of each institution produced several structures of budgeting and accounting. Indeed, each region has its own accounting law (see Table 3.5).

Regions were also able to adopt their own internal accounting regulation, adapting national rules to their own needs to a limited extent. As a consequence, the system is very heterogeneous. Indeed, there are strong differences, not only between different entities of local government, but also between local and central governments in terms of accounting arrangements (Mussari, 2012). In consideration of heterogeneity between the different levels of government and its self-governing powers, IPSAS have been poorly implemented in Italy (Megali & Pozzoli, 2003; Caccia & Steccolini, 2006; Grossi & Soverchia, 2011) given the remarkable extension of these standards and the present trend toward harmonization. Nevertheless, in this recent reform, any reference to IPSAS principles has been retrieved.

The Italian reforms of public accounting systems were characterized by the adoption of different approaches to the type of administration that induced coordination significant problems (Borgonovi, 2005; Anselmi & Ponzo, 2009). Conversely, the reform process is based on the adoption of a unique system, one that was extended to the entire variegated universe of government, which currently employs accounting systems and financial statements which are not coincident (Bisogno, 2008) (Table 4.5).

4.8 Campania Region, the First Year of Trial

Campania is a region of southern Italy (see Table 3.4), which includes five provinces: Naples, Caserta, Salerno, Benevento, and Avellino. The institutional arrangement of the Campania Region is as follows: *The Regional Committee* (Giunta Regionale), which has government powers. It is composed of 11 councils or sand headed by the president of the region, The *Regional Council* (Consiglio Regionale), which has

Table 4.5 Italian regions in the trial

Location	Region	Flags	Status	Accounting regulation	Participation in the trial
North	Aosta Valley		Autonomous	Regional Law 16/1992	No
North	Piedmont		Ordinary	Regional Law 7/2001	No
North	Lombardy		Ordinary	Regional Law 27/2000	Yes, selected by the Ministry
North	Trentino-South Tyrol		Autonomous	Regional Law 10/1991	No
North	Friuli-Venezia Giulia		Autonomous	Regional Law 7/1999	No
North	Veneto		Ordinary	Regional Law 39/2001	No
North	Liguria		Ordinary	Regional Law 15/2002	Yes, voluntarily
North	Emilia Romagna		Ordinary	Regional Law 40/2001	No
Center	Tuscany		Ordinary	Regional Law 36/2001	Yes, voluntarily
Center	Marche		Ordinary	Regional Law 31/2001	No
Center	Umbria		Ordinary	Regional Law 13/2000	No
Center	Lazio		Ordinary	Regional Law 25/2001	Yes, selected by the Ministry
Center	Abruzzo		Ordinary	Regional Law 3/2002	No
South	Molise		Ordinary	Regional Law 4/2002	No
South	Campania		Ordinary	Regional Law 7/2002	Yes, selected by the Ministry
South	Basilicata		Ordinary	Regional Law 34/2001	Yes, selected by the Ministry

(continued)

Table 4.5 (continued)

Location	Region	Flags	Status	Accounting regulation	Participation in the trial
South	Apulia		Ordinary	Regional Law 28/2001	No
South	Calabria		Ordinary	Regional Law 8/2002	No
South	Sicily		Autonomous	Regional Law 6/2001	No
South	Sardinia	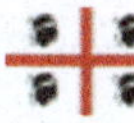	Autonomous	Regional Law 23/1999	No

legislative powers. The Campania region was composed of 61 directors, divided into ten-member boards.

Recently, the offices of the Campania Region were reorganized (with resolution no. 427 of 27 September 2013)[6]: designation of five General Managers; organization of the Staff Structures to the Department and to the General Management.

There are five General Managers who direct five Departments, divided into the following areas:

- Planning and economic development;
- Healthcare and Natural Resources;
- Territorial policies;
- Education, research, work, cultural, and social policies;

Financial, human, and material resources (Fig. 4.2).

Regarding the accounting arrangements, the trial of the harmonization reform officially began with a series of start-up measures. Specifically, the Regional Committee sent an official note (n. 780 of 29th December 2011) to the Ministry of Economy and Finance, which identifies two instrumental organizations to be involved in the trial. These include the Agency for work and education (Agenzia per il lavoro e l'istruzione) and the Health Local Organization (Azienda Sanitaria Locale) in Avellino. The Regional Decree of the President of the Region Campania, n. 255 of 15 November 2011, identified the figures within the organization who are responsible for implementing the measures contained in the reform. This included those responsible for the trial and a working group[7] in the Department Financial, and human and material resources.

[6]http://www.beta.regione.campania.it/it/regione. Appendix "D" to the Regional Council of Deliberation n. 528 of 04/10/2012 amendment to the Regional Council Resolution no. 478/2012.

[7]Responsible of trial: dr. Giulio Mastracchio; now replaced by Dr. Maria Salerno; Dr. Bruno Rosati, General Manager of the Department; Dr. Fortuna Gabriella Acciarino; Dr. Giulia Migliore; and Dr. Maria Simonetti. All the members of the Department have been very open to accept train sheep

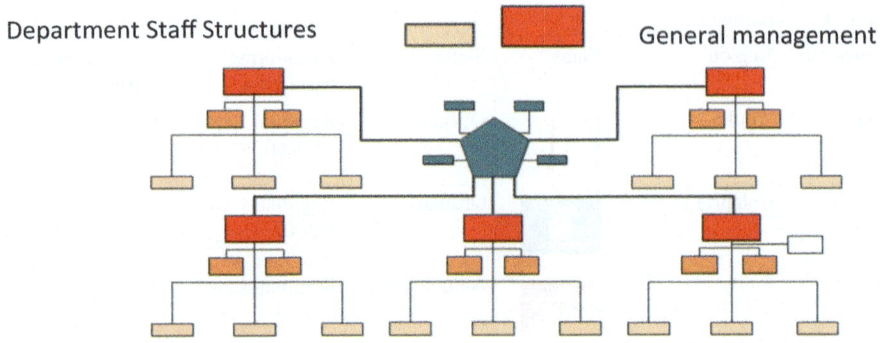

Fig. 4.2 Campania region, the organization chart. *Source* From Regional Council of Deliberation n. 528 of 4th October 2012, Appendix D

In the same Regional Decree the Campania Region, according to the art. n. 2, paragraph 4, of Legislative Decree 118/2011, the implementation of accrual accounting was postponed. The integrated chart of accounts and the consolidated financial statements give priority to annual budget reform measures, which is perceived as an essential tool for the planning, management, and reporting activities. At this point, it is important to remember that in Campania region accrual accounting has never been implemented. However, the region has fulfilled other measures of the reform on time. The first of these was a new budget structure (Bruno, 2013).

It has already anticipated that the budget of the regions should be structured according to the state budget harmonization reform in *missions* and *programs* and that it be consistent with the classification (COFOG) applied in the EU. The previous structure of the Campania Region budget (according to the art. 17 of the Regional accounting Law n. 7 of 30 April 2002) was articulated in *Areas of Intervention* and *objective functions* (Funzionio obiettivo) that represented institutional missions pursued. *Base Unit Projections* (Unità previsionali di base) were defined, according to the different purposes of expenditure, in relation to the character binding or mandatory spending and in relation to the differences in economic structure. In operational reality, at least with regard to the Campania Region, the reclassification process was carried out for "aggregations progressive", starting from individual *chapters (Capitoli),* the smaller classification which have been traced back to the missions and programs, to ensure consistency with the COFOG classification.

The Campania region, since 2007, had begun to explore standardization of balance sheet items. The Decree n. 17114 of 5th March 2007 contains provisions for the international classification of government expenditure by function, and it clarifies how and when to implement the SIOPE for the regions. This document was attached to the financial statements for the years 2010 and 2011. This documentation was required for an initial verification of compatibility between existing economic and

organized in collaboration with the University Department, so that it was possible to access the data, in a special way the supervisor, Dr. Silvana Grasso.

functional classification systems. It also addressed the new classifications, and SIOPE COFOG views its introduction in the regional budget.

With Decree n. 159 by the Regional Committee on March 28th 2012, the Ministry also recommended the adoption of a new financial statement.

The annual budget was sent to the working group Arconet. The responsible for trial received an assessment notification that emphasized that the Campania region was the first among the three regions in that trial that had fully responded to the structure of the formats required by the new law.

Regarding the reform of the healthcare accounting system, the professional promoter involved in the trial is a KPMG partner. He was appointed (Regional Decree n. 227 of 10th of October 2012) to be the official consultant for the centralization management of the health sector system and the implementation of the integrated accrual accounting system. In particular, KPMG studied the health-management cycle in terms of the principles of accrual accounting started to analyze the financial transactions used to implement the new system (Bruno, 2014). The Campania Region under Decree n. 277 of 10th October 2012 approved the new Integrated Chart of Accounts of Regional Health Authorities (GSA). An aspect that deserves attention is that during the observation period the KPMG consultant participated in the video conference call and in the institutional meeting with the working group. KPMG played the leading role, in both processes due to their advantage and expertise.

4.9 Research Method

In this research, policy documents are used as primary sources because they provide almost all or a majority of the data needed for this contemporary social research. Policy documents are also used as important resources for data triangulation, to increase the comprehensiveness and validity of the single case study. Indeed, in a qualitative research documentary analysis, this is useful to permit an in-depth understanding (Patton, 2002).

In most instances to conduct an analysis of documents, the literature identifies two different approaches, which are as follows:

- The *content analysis* is the analysis of documents for their content;
- The *context analysis* is the traditional method used for policy document analysis to investigate how the document produces events or phenomena (Yin, 2009).

The Content analysis is useful as a typical method for inductive analysis. It is used is to "identify core consistencies and meanings (Patton, 2002, p. 453)". In this kind of analysis, external source attention is minimal (Miller &Alvarado, 2005). The *context analysis* has been further strengthened by a longitudinal perspective, which is essential to understanding the research context (Prior, 2003). This analysis is aimed at collecting laws and internal rules related to the harmonization process under the trial. It has conducted an initial overview of the Italian reform process by collecting published parliamentary documents related to the Italian public sector reform process and the development of accrual accounting. More specifically, the data collected for documentary analysis are policy documents (laws, accounting rules, and committee resolution) on a central and regional level (Table 3.3). Alternatively, *the Context analysis* is described as "ethnographic", because when adopting this approach, documents are studied as elements, which result from social activity. In this field, it is possible to find two possible approaches:

- *Documents as commentary*: The analysis of documents as commentary in literature is the most utilized in the qualitative studies, which adopt a case study to interpret the reality described in the documents. For example, it could be used when describing the institutional structure in the traditional policy documents. It is also useful in asking questions, such as "how" and "why" (Yin, 2009). The descriptive orientation is predominant. In most cases, the documents as commentary analysis are employed in the analysis of the relationship between policy and practice. It focuses on one of the "gaps" between theory and practice. These studies about policy and organization change are mostly ex post oriented.
- *Documents as actors*: This is a distinct approach utilized by researchers who adopt a *constructivist view*. In other words, "the social reality is generated by the interaction of human and nonhuman as a consequence documents are actors or actants (Latour & Woolgar, 1979) in the social field" (Miller & Alvarado, 2005, p. 351). This kind of perspective is able to shed light on the complexity of policy-making the negotiation and translation developed in practice.

In this analysis, we followed the document *in use*, to analyze how these policies are constructed according to *logical text analysis* (Latour, 1987). The core aspect of this process is focusing on how documents are inscribed to produce phenomena. The local conditions of its production are less important (Miller, 1997; Prior, 2003; Miller & Alvarado, 2005). In this research, if it is followed a more distinctive analytical method in which it is considered *how policy documents*, from 2009 until 2012, *were constructed* by adopting the *fortification tactics of texts* of Latour. The process of constructing policy documents is used to investigate the role played by social forces. The first concept deployed in this analysis is *stacking*. This entails scrutiny of the issues related to "accrual accounting", looking at how this is expressed over the time and covered, step by step, year by year. To find traces of "stacking" characteristics requires access to policies' texts that explain with temporal coherency, accrual accounting, following the timeline, as it would occur in a book chapter. The *staging* and *framing* strategies were also considered in the analysis. In this case, we investigated the absence or presence of technical data related to the implementation, tabulation, examples, and details for accrual accounting implementation. Furthermore, we consider *captation*, the subtle control of implementers. Specifically, if there is *captation*, there is a clear single path for implementers and "wandering paths" are avoided.

In this research, the question related to the policy is "What if, instead of policy-producing practice, practices, produce policy? (Mosse, 2004)". In this research, the analysis is ex ante because it looks not only at policy development, and its effect but also at how the development works, opening the block box. This is an attempt to open the black box that exists between policy prescriptions in one area as well as its effects on another. The focus is not on "whether policy is implemented", but on "how the design is in practice" (Mosse, 2004, p. 141).

To summarize, the most important things which have been included in a research design are shown in the five questions and answers elaborated by Pratt, the "Checklist of Questions to Be Addressed in Qualitative Methods" (Pratt, 2008, p. 504).

1. Why this study? Because we found the gap in literature regarding the ex ante studies.
    a. Why are qualitative methods appropriate? Because we are adopting the Constructionism/Ethnographic approach instead of a Positivism/Mainstream approach.
    b. Am I building, elaborating, or testing theory? Our objective is a theoretical abstraction.
2. Why study here? Because Italy is at the initial stage of implementation of an accrual accounting system in governments.
    a. What is the nature of the context I am examining? We are examining the intermediate level of government, the region.
    b. What was my rationale for choosing this context? The region never implemented an accrual accounting system, so it is possible to investigate the construction process.
3. What am I studying and why? We are studying the implementation of an accrual accounting system in government. Accrual accounting in the public sector is considered self-evident by NPM advocates. However, the studies about its complexity are still a challenge for a researcher. We want to enrich our understanding, adopting an ex ante perspective.
    a. Am I sampling events, cases, people, etc.? This is an explorative research and we adopt two methods of data collection, policy document, and video conference call, in-site non-participant observations.
    b. What is my sampling strategy? We chose one of the four regions involved in the trial of the accounting reform, the Campania Region. This region has never implemented an accrual accounting system.
4. How did I study these things? Opening Pandora's Black Box. By trying to give up all the stereotypes related to accrual accounting, and entering for the first time into the laboratory life.
    a. How did we analyze the data? By analyzing the policy documents and the reports of the video call conversations as a blueprint.
    b. How did I link data with theory? In this analysis, we followed the document *in use*, to analyze how these it was constructed according to conducting a *logical text analysis* by Latour (1987). In this way, we have highlighted all

Table 4.6 Involvement by research phase

Aproximate Period Covered	2011	2012	2013
Research Characteristic	Historical	Various formal interviews	Management information accounting group
Documentation	■	■	■
Formal interview		■	■
Formal Meetings			■
In site observation			■
Videocall			■
Transcription devices			
Fields notes		■	■
Audio Tapes		■	■

the interpretations, machinations, and fabrications, created by flaws in the policy documents. So it turns out they are fabrications in accrual accounting.

Lastly, in this table, it is summarized the involvement in terms of time of the researcher and the transcription devices utilized for the data collection (Table 4.6).

Chapter 5
Results of Documentary Analysis Policy Arenas

Abstract This chapter contains partial research results, specifically, results from the documentary analysis. According to the theoretical framework and the chosen methodological approach, the results of this research are the systematization of the artifacts, which appear during the accrual accounting construction. Accrual accounting is canonically recognized by private sector as systematic practice for reporting the results of the company (Potito, 1973). Throughout these chapters, this research will illustrate that this knowledge is not well established and defined in the public sector. Indeed, accrual accounting is distorted during its translation to the public sector. These results are obtained from primordial applications of the new technology, because the trial is still ongoing. In Italy, this trial is called "Experimentation" (Sperimentazione). Experimentation is defined by Bachelard as "Experts, equipped with instruments to follow the *collective experiment* in a controlled environment" (Bachelard, 2007). Thus, we will have analyzed the collective action before and after the policy document was composed. The material elements that constitute the foundation of the accrual accounting system in the public sector are laws, tools (ICT), designers, and implementers. Indeed, to understand how this system translates into the public economic and financial system requires us to examine its *text features*, which reveal its original framework. Accrual accounting gets the highest degree of forma legitimacy from the Decree 118/2011. However, in the decree, the definition of accrual accounting plays a marginal role. As a consequence, the trial attempts to explain and analyze how accrual accounting is put into practice in a public setting, as have recent books, conferences, and seminars (both in academia and in the institutional context) on the topic.

5.1 Human and Non-Human Actors

"Construction of a new technology" and the accrual accounting engineering process include both.[1]

---

[1]**Gaston Bachelard** was a French philosopher. He made contributions in the fields of poetics and the philosophy of science. He rose to some of the most prestigious positions in

A. Bruno, *New Public Management (NPM) and the Introduction of an Accrual Accounting System*, SpringerBriefs in Accounting,
https://doi.org/10.1007/978-3-030-57386-7_5

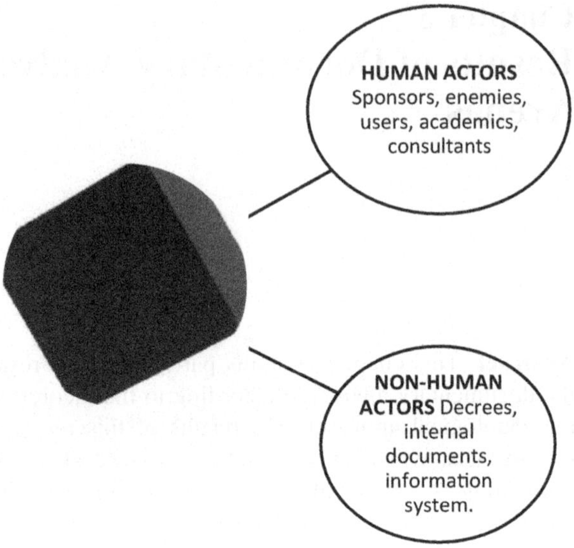

Fig. 5.1 The fabrication process of a black box

- *Non-human actors*, such as decrees, law, standards, implementation tools, and codes. These will be underlined the partial and inaccurate information contained in the policy, the blueprint.
- *Human actors*, including users, consultants, academics, sponsors, allies, and enemies who are attempting to build a new technology based on these policies, which are not a blueprint, as we will see in this chapter (Fig. 5.1).

Human and non-human actors team up participate in the construction process. The negotiations and controversies of two groups give rise to artifacts. Analyzing these controversies about the nature of accrual accounting, we are opening the black box (Latour, 1987). As we underlined in Chap. 2, the black box is accepted and taken for granted. It is adopted without discussion by the actors involved. However, opening the black box, we will show that the accrual accounting implementation in governments gives rise to numerous discussions.

Thus, if we want to investigate construction and translation process related to accrual accounting system in government, it is appropriate to start at the time human actors first enroll and then analyze their influence on the process of policy construction. We first analyzed the documents related to the process, specifically, looking at content based on the assumption that the policy was used as a blueprint. Adopting the theoretical framework of technoscience, we will explain how some dictations contained in the decree, which call on regional and local governments to adopt a single accounting language and harmonious and an accrual accounting system, have

the Académiefrançaise and influenced many subsequent French philosophers, among them Michel Foucault and Jacques Derrida.

Fig. 5.2 The policy path

been translated into practice. For a better understanding, the stages of policy development are graphically represented following the logical and temporal sequences of a blueprint (Fig. 5.2).

The *implementation phase*, which in this study we prefer to define as the translation[2] phase, should not lead to a distortion from input to output. Actors in this phase should simply translate the content developed in the *decision phase* into practice. If that were the case, the policy would be a blueprint. However, many studies have demonstrated the *non-linearity of this process*. For example, studies of public choice, which are premised on rationality, are focused on the policy cycle. The interpretative models that study the implementation phase have revealed incomplete action cycles and a gap between policies as they designed and how they eventually emerge (Hoffman, 1997; Mueller, 2008). This study seeks to expand on that point. However, this study will look at the translation phase as *a construction practice*, with emergence status using the theoretical background of Latour's approach.

Before analyzing the implementation process, it is necessary to consider the decision phase (Fig. 4.2). This is the information that is supposed to be used during the implementation. In this section, we will analyze how the text of the Policy is changed and added onto immediately before becoming decree. This will reveal the influence of the political component before the box becomes black.

There are three fundamental assumptions in this analysis:

- the *implementer* (the bureaucrat, the employees) is considered as the party who *interprets* the policies, translates them, betraying, filling the silence, altering the final stage;
- the *politician*, the Ministry, the legislator is the party who *expresses his will in a legislative text*, which can be issued as a law, a decree, or a circular;
- the *policies are a script*[3] which guides the human actors in proper implementation of accrual accounting. The script, as defined by computer science, is a *list of commands*, formulated with a specific syntax, called scripting language. In this study, the policies are the script for the construction of a new technology, the accrual accounting.

Policies have to get to the material consistency, an accrual accounting system. We will demonstrate that these policies are not a blueprint but a *technological artifact* because they allow a number of alternative uses in preconceived contexts. Accrual

---

[2]Translation indicates also a geometric shift from one phase to another.

[3]Scripts are applied to computer programs designed to interpret a sequence of lines of text which may be entered by a user, read from a file or another kind of data stream. The context of interpretation is usually one of a given operating system or programming language. Source: https://en.wikipedia.org/wiki/Command_line_interpreter#Command-line_interpreter.

accounting is an instrument designed to transport the intentions of whoever writes the information and participates in the decision and implementation process (politicians, employees, academics, consultants, member of committees). It is not a neutral technology.

5.2 The First Enrollment of Human Actors: The Arenas of the Policy

Latour describes the concept of translation by using the metaphor of *the rugby match* in which the players involved pass the ball to each other (Latour, 1987, p. 104). Similarly, in this study we look at the process of construction of accrual accounting as a rugby match, analyzing the steps and positions that the players/actors assume and their trajectories. We are analyzing how the ball (the policy) is passed from hand to hand (institutional actors) until they achieve the goal. We will specifically look at who goes ahead or those who try to shut down its path, and who is compelled to pass it on to others. The actors are involved in shaping the policy; therefore, they are the *multi-conductor.* They draw it. They modify it. They alter it. Adopting Latour's theory, it is possible to look at the actors involved in the construction of accrual accounting, which are those described in this circle (which could be seen as a rugby ball). The circle also represents the arena of institutional actors involved in the first phase of policy construction, the input, and the third phase of the policy, the output (Fig. 5.3).

Fig. 5.3 The circle of actors

First are analyzed ***the politics actors*** involved in the construction. The first actor is the Ministry of Economy and Finance, which presents the first act (339) to the Chamber of Deputy, specifically to the Budget Committee of the Chamber of Deputy Research Department.

In Italy, the Ministry of Economy and Finance is the executive body responsible for financial, economic, and budget policy.[4] In the case of public accounting reform, the Ministry is the proponent of the policy, which is a Legislative Decree. Indeed in the Italian legislative system, the Legislative Decree is a legislative measure which has the force of law once adopted by the executive power (the government) after the explicit and formal delegation of legislative power (Parliament). There are similar legislative acts in other countries, for example, in Spain (decreto con fuerza de ley), in France (ordonnance), or in United States (executive orders). Specifically, in Italy, the Chambers decide to not focus on the detail of given subject, due to either technical inadequacies or lack of time, but will establish a framework (principles and criteria) to allow the Government to legislate. Thus, the Legislative Decrees taken in areas reserved for statute law but they are secondary legislation specifically authorized by Law. That law is called "enabling law" or "application decrees", which are approved by both Houses, similar to any other law, but define implementation details for the decree. Specifically, the decree regulates the scope, the guidelines, and the limits to which the government must abide when preparing the Legislative Decrees. In this case, the Law n. 42/2009 contained the delegation to the Ministry calling on it to prepare a Legislative Decree about public sector accounting reform. The Minister prepares this act, subordinating it to the parliamentary counsel.

Upon request of parliamentary groups, the Budget Committee provides advice to the parliamentary bodies. This Committee is also composed of politicians. In this case, the Research Departments of the Committee published the report, which will be analyzed in the next section. Another political entity is also involved in the nation-wide accounting system reform, the *United Conference State-Regions*. This group is composed of regional representatives. The Prime Minister is the president, which has strengthened its advisory functions. The conference advises on general guidelines related to legislation that is of direct interest to the regions and local governments. Specifically, the mission of this conference is to represent the specific interests of local and regional governments. As a consequence, it is a required part of the regional and inter-regional decision-making processes. The reform analyzed in this section is no exception.

We also analyze the ***technical actors involved*** in this process: the *State General Accounting Department* (Ragioneria Generale delloStato), which is the technical section of the Ministry of Economy and Finance, the *Supreme Audit institution* (Corte dei Conti), which retains some responsibility as advisory to the Ministry of Economy and Finance and the *Committees for fiscal federalism* (Commissione per il federalism fiscal). The institutional mission of the State General Accounting Department is to "support the Parliament and the Government on budget policies, processes and

[4]Source: https://www.tesoro.it/en/ministero/di-piu-mef/missione.html.

procedures".[5] The primary institutional objective of the Department is to guarantee the accurate administration and the rigorous planning and programming of public resources. It also draws the annual draft of the national budget and draft and monitors public expenditures. Recently, the Department's functions were extended in order to allow for the public sector accounting reform implementation. It was already specified in the research context chapter that State General Accounting Department has the main role in this construction process as a facilitator, guide, decision-maker, and controller. There is an entire department dedicated to the reform, specifically to the trial (Arconet). In addition, a conference has been organized[6] to present the reform to the entities. A special issue of a national journal whose users are for the most part the civil servants[7] has also been entirely dedicated to it.

The *Committee for fiscal federalism* is an established component of the Ministry of Economy and Finance and operates within the United Conference State-Regions. The mission is to satisfy the information needs of the policy-makers and regional and local governments through consultative activities. The committee is composed of politicians, academics, and consultants. Thus ***consultants*** and ***academics*** play a role in the match as well. Specifically, in the *translating of interest game* (Callon, 1986), it will be clear as the Committee plays a "tackles[8]".

Regarding the academics, there has been speculation about the outcomes, which have been advanced by Italian scholars. Specifically, in a special issue of an Italian journal dedicated to the reform, an Italian professor who is a consultant to the Committee for Fiscal Federalism wrote that:

> the process of construction of the new accounting system and the budget will be studied closely. These are the reasons: the doubts and the different interpretations of Legislative Decree no. 118/2011 and the declared opposition from regions about some accounting solutions proposed in the policy, particularly the accrual accounting system (Mussari, 2012, p. 15).
>
> In particular, the regions more prominently than the local governments have so far not regulated and set up an accounting approach of an economic nature which is adjustable to the standardization of costs (D'Alessio, 2012, p. 29).

Prof. Pozzoli clarifies that to write in the text of the decree that the accrual accounting must be introduced *for cognitive purpose* was a mistake because

> …an accounting system must to have meaning, it cannot be a tinsel,…(Pozzoli, 2012, p. 79).

---

[5] Source: https://www.rgs.mef.gov.it/ENGLISH-VE/The-State-/about-us/Department-of-General-Accounts.html.

[6] https://www.rgs.mef.gov.it/VERSIONE-I/e-GOVERNME1/ARCONET/videoconvegno/index.html.

[7] Finanza locale, n. 3 2013.

[8] In rugby, the primary purposes of tackling are to dispossess an opponent of the ball, to stop the player from gaining ground toward goal or to stop them from carrying out what they intend. Source https://en.wikipedia.org/wiki/Tackle_(football_move).

Information that emerged from the previous meeting has pointed out that:

> the decree **is somewhat ambiguous about the mandatory or not of such a system.** In other words, if the purpose it will be purely cognitive or it will represent the basis for reporting and if it will affect also the consolidated financial statements, which should be obtainable on the actual cost and on the outsourced services. It is reported as well as **the ambiguity of the function**, the lack - and this is a gap that should be absolutely filled - of correlation between accrual accounting and standard costs, which should be the main purpose be attributed to this instrument in the new federal structure.

Thus, for the Committee, the text of the decree, in its current form appears **to be evasive on crucial points**. It is not clear enough to guide the testing methodologies to default. Then, on p. 17, the same deputy points out the *contradictions in the text of the decree*, specifically ones related to the introduction of accrual accounting and balance sheet. As was revealed in the hearings, the text of the decree is **ambiguous about the mandatory nature** of such a system; in other words, if it is introduced for cognitive purpose, it is not clear whether or not the system will provide the basis for reporting.

During the meeting of 1st of June 2011, there is a request for a clarification of the draft decree and the decree approved some days before (Legislative Decree 31 May 2011). The clarification request concerns the accounting harmonization of the State, which is derived from the Law 196 of the 2009. In addition, it reports the following paragraphs about the trial, which is from the memorandum issued by Marco Causi, member of Chamber of Deputy:

> There are two requirements which have to be satisfied; the first is about the trial. The trial should be referred to the widest possible number of entities, such as, all the municipalities above 5,000 inhabitants. Moreover it has been considered to request to the State General Accounting Department a formal Note about **the comparability between the text** of the decree in question and the Decree on the harmonization of accounting systems for the central government, approved by the Government yesterday, in order to assess **the consistency** between the two measures (Copaff, 2011, p. 60).

The deputy Linda LANZILLOTTA also considers

> the necessity to extend as much as possible the new rule for the financial statements to local authorities, otherwise, **the trial** combined with the existing accounting system, **would be reduced to a mere academic exercise** (Copaff, 2011, p. 61).

During the last meeting of 8th of June before the release, the Committee requests, among other things, the integration and modification of the text in some parts, more specifically.

> Integration on the Article 4, paragraph 2, after the words: in order to add the following: highlight, through the applied accounting principles, the process of connection, even in a timeline, the economic and financial data (Copaff, 2011, p. 514).
>
> in order to **a better quality of text**, the government should carry out a **formal review of the overall scheme**, as well as designations in it contains, in particular by standardizing those related to the financial statements (Copaff, 2011, p. 518).
>
> assess the opportunity to provide that the trial of **accrual accounting** should occur through the adoption of the method of **double-entry bookkeeping** (Copaff, 2011, p. 518);

In May 2011, there is an Audition by the *Supreme Audit Institution* (Corte dei Conti, Audizione sullo schema di d.lgs. n. 339 recante disposizioni per l'attuazione dell'articolo 2, comma 2, lettera h) della legge 5 maggio 2009, n. 42 e successive modificazioni). In the text, there are general considerations about the reform of public sector accounting.

A general consideration is as follows:

> Over more than three decades the attempts made in this direction have had, as is well known, **scarce success** (Corte dei Conti, 2011, p. 5)]..[This current complex operation **is not without practical difficulties**. Some problems especially **referring to regional governments where accounting systems are variously articulated** (Corte dei Conti, 2011, p. 6).
>
> For implementation process, is of crucial importance the coverage of information and technology needs, which requires the strengthening of **automation on informative systems**......](Corte dei Conti, 2011, p. 7).

As a general consideration, *the Supreme Audit Institution, continuing saying* that

> the terms contained on the article 35, paragraph 2, which the decree authorizes the trial mode **even as an exception to the existing disciplines accounting are puzzling.** Therefore **is necessary to delete the phrase**; even if, the general will is to give most content in the trial instead to the previous legislation, **the wording should be amended**. (Corte dei Conti, 2011, p. 13).

The report of the Supreme Audit Institution continues with an evaluation of the principles and postulates described in the text of the decree.

> One aspect that should be carefully **evaluated concerns the principles and the general criteria, which are a direct pronouncement**....] [This is a set fairly circumscribed definition of consolidated rules statements contained in Annex 1 of the Decree, which identifies 18 "General Principles or postulates."(Corte dei Conti, 2011, p. 12). The attachment is made up of eighteen accounting policies that largely reproduce the content of the postulates concerning the budget system of local authorities, approved Observatory for the finance and accounting of local authorities (12 March 2008) that, turn, found their inspiration in the most significant document n. 11 of the National Standard Setter for the Company (OIC) - Financial Statements - Purposes and postulates.
>
> Their substantial derivation from the accounting principles adopted by the National Standard Setter (OIC) may require, sometimes, **specific adaptations to the features of the accounting system of public administrations.**
>
> Specifically, referring to **an accrual basis of accounting**, in which the identification of several criteria of allocation of accounting entries, depending on whether it's costs and revenues (refer to exchange processes that occur in the market) or of income and expenses (attributable to assets institutional and/or grant-making) **is formulated in terms lexically confused and sometimes lack of logical consistency**. Similarly, is not entirely clear whether the omitted specification of the evaluation criteria public art. 2 schema it means an implicit referring to the principles of the Civil Code (Article 2423-bis, n. 6). (Corte dei Conti, 2011, p. 19).

In May 2011, the Research Department of the Senate of the Republic analyzes the text of the decree, spreading a report, the Act n. 359, n. 47 of May 2011 (Senato della Reppublica, 2011).

The report, regarding the principles which each administration has to apply, specifies that in paragraph 2 of the decree, the accounting regulation of each public administration should be consistent with **the principles contained in the Appendix 1**. However, "the original text of draft 339 **referred also** to take in consideration the main national practice indicated by the Italian Accounting **(OIC),** and the Observatory for the accounting of local authorities (OEL) and the international accounting issued by the **International Public Sector Accounting Standards Board (IPSAS) by the International Accounting Standards Board (IPSASB),** as compatible with the new rules on accounting and public finance.**This prediction has been replaced by a more limited consistency** with the accounting policies set out in the diagram in Appendix 1 (Senato della Reppublica, 2011, p. 11).

A whole section of this report is dedicated to the **criticality of the implementation of accrual accounting.** Many critical issues are in fact related to the application of the matching principle of accounting. Specifically,

Generally, for manufacturing companies, the timing for accounting entry is: during the purchase, upon receipt of the invoice of the goods purchased and during the sale, the time of issuance of the bill of sale. At the end of the reporting period, after making the accounting entries of integration and adjustment, it will calculate the net income of the year. By contrast, in public sector, regardless of the specificity of the classes of companies, the budget is made up of chapters where are the estimates of expenditure and revenue expected can be made in terms of cash. The result at the end of the reporting year is a surplus or deficit spending. On first analysis, although the two settings appear simple and linear, it is undeniable **that many would seem the obstacles and difficulties that interposed in the path of integration and harmonization of the two accounting systems.**

Referring to public accounting, it is deeply linked to the procedural moments of public administrations activities; the main purpose of public accounting is to ensure the ex-ante consistency of use of resources according to the purpose. By contrast, the priority of accrual accounting is usually the ex-post measurement of management which has produced - in terms of flow (income) and/or stock (equity), influencing the profit or loss for the year]...[It is evident the potential of the accrual accounting system in the measurement of the value produced in a reporting year, but at the same time there **is an high level of discretion in this evaluation method**. Indeed, it is reiterated that **the main problem related to the implementation of an accounting system** in public entities is not the classification of budgetary data but is **the time recording and the different criteria of which set the accounting entries have to done in during the management process.** Indeed, as is well known, **in a public accounting system** what is relevant is the **legal effect of the transactions;** by contrast in a***n accrual accounting system*** what is relevant is **the information dimension** of the transactions, where is important to differentiate the impacts on income and equity.]....[In other words, the adoption of an accrual accounting system **requires a decisive "cultural" change in public sector**, because in addition to legal and administrative expenditure profiles it will be necessary **to detect the "interpretation" aspects on the nature of expenses**, as flow or stock] (Senato della Reppublica, 2011, p. 18).

The same report also comments on the formulation of the matching principle of accounting. It outlines.

a range of transactions do not appear in the principle, that refers to events that occur but in terms chronologically very "distant" from their financial dynamic (for example exceptional/extraordinary losses and write downs of assets/downward adjustment of income), and other where is does not exist the financial accounting record.

In the report, there is a section devoted to the preparation of the integrated chart of accounts.

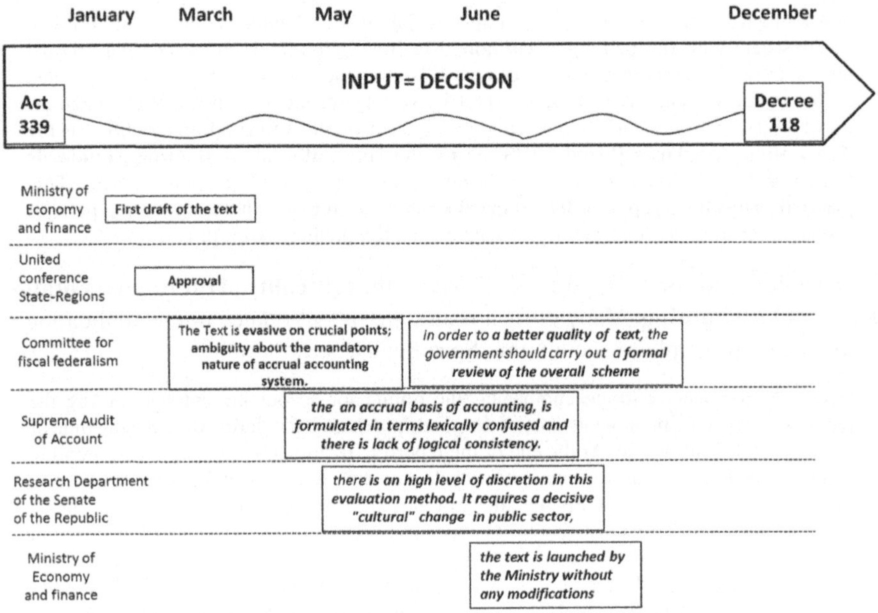

Fig. 5.4 Non-linearity in the decision path

> [... In this regard, it should highlight the paragraphs that defines the chart of accounts as a list of the accounts of accrual and financial, created to allow a detailed analysis of each entries. However, **generally the construction of a chart of accounts is typically preceded by a prior identification of information needs** which have to comply with the accounting data] (Senato della Reppublica, 2011, p. 25).

Since the rule requires the simultaneous recognition both financial and accrual accounting, the report focuses on typical accrual entries, the adjusting entries, including depreciation, accrual, and prepayment calculations.

> [paragraph 2 expressly provides the implementation of the operations of recording typical accrual accounting, bookkeeping depreciation, adjusting entries; regarding this aspect, it is also necessary **to stress once again** the limit significance of repeatedly mentioned as "**discretionary evaluation**" in particular way, where the same results are then used for the purposes of policy evaluation of public finance] (Senato della Reppublica, 2011, p. 35).

The official text of the decree was published on June 23, 2011. The text is now in its third version because during the trial, it had been modified.[10] These steps are resumed in Fig. 4.4 (Fig. 5.4).

Figure 5.4 shows a temporal flowing, of the parts of the reports of the committees that have amended the text of 339, which later became the text of Decree 118. To

[10]The last version has been published on 3rd of March 2014, source: www.rgs.mef.gov.it/VERSIONE-I/e-GOVERNME1/ARCONET/

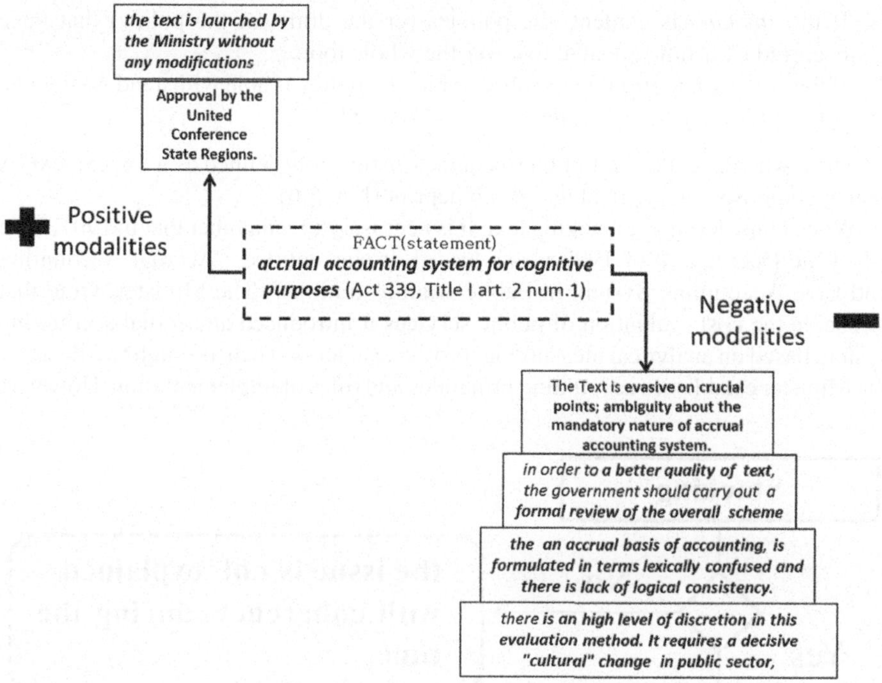

Fig. 5.5 Policy's modalities

analyze these texts by adopting Latour's approach, these components become positive or negative *modalities* (see page 27, Chap. 2) that scientists (politicians, members of Committee) try to push in the direction of fact.

- There are *positive modalities* if there is *confirmation*,
- There are *negative modalities* if we have *skeptical assertions.*

So starting from the text, from the statement which specifies the ***accrual accounting system for cognitive purposes*** Act 339, Title I art. 2 num.1, we have four negative modalities and two positive modalities (Fig. 5.5).

5.4 Policy as a Blueprint

As mentioned earlier, a blueprint is a sequence of logic procedures that enables the construction of a technology. *So, this leads us to the following question: Is a policy is a blueprint?* Latour individuates four strategies for writing a text as a blueprint (see Chap. 2). These techniques are defined as *positioning tactics*. A *blueprint policy* does not leave space to the *assault of readers*, in other words, the production of negative modalities, for the following reasons:

1. If the *stacking* is evident, the policies (or the drafts of the policy) that have occurred over time are able to cover the whole topic.
2. If the *staging* and *framing* are observable, the policy is able withstand dissidents.
3. If the *captation* is visible, the policy is armored.

Thus, when a text has all of these characteristics, it is defined as a logical text. A policy composed of a logical text is a blueprint (Fig. 5.6).

When considering the stacking text, it is necessary to remember that in 1997, Title III of the Decree 279 of 1997 was released. It was entitled: "Accrual Accounting and Cost Accounting System in Public Administrations". The Minister wrote that to enable the cost evaluation of public services it introduced an accrual accounting system based on analytical measurements by cost centers. Then, through two decrees, the Minister establishes accounting principles and rules of implementation. However,

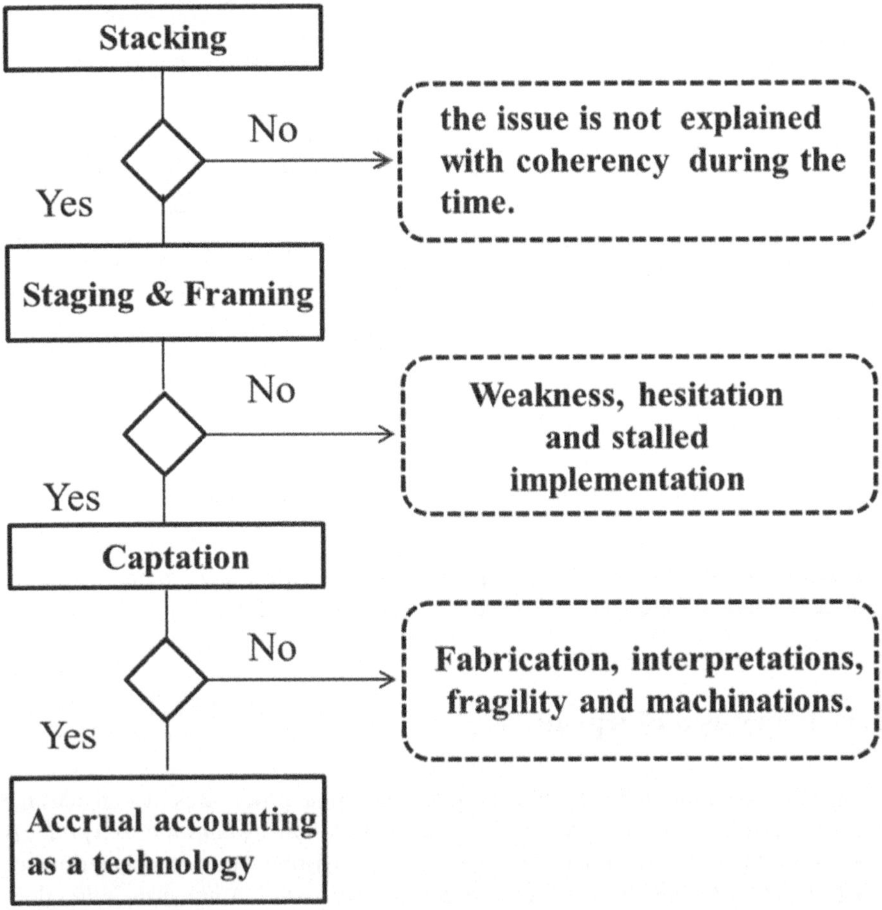

Fig. 5.6 Policy as blueprint

this system is introduced without any reform of the accounting system, so it is a complementary instrument that has to integrate the pre-existing system. For many years, implementation has been stalled, so it is reasonable to declare that the stacking in the different policies was not done well.

The other characteristics that enable a policy to become a blueprint are *framing* and *staging*. This means anticipating that the reader may raise objections or suggest course changes. For example, the document might add some examples of the implementation of accrual accounting. Referring to this aspect, the Committee for fiscal federalism wrote that *in order to create **a better quality of text**, the government should carry out a **formal review of the overall scheme**.*

Even if the policy includes a huge amount of technical data, it may not be sufficient if the reader has the chance to walk and to wander through the document. All the *movements* should be controlled in some way; otherwise, it may experience a high degree of defeats. This leads to the question: What parts of the text might leave the reader completely free, and which parts help to maintain obedience? What is the solution to this paradox? The solution is to draw the text in such a way that the reader has only one way to go. But can this be accomplished, if from the beginning the reader is left free to follow any direction? It's easy to understand, making it more difficult the rest of the *roads*, and build topics which are *hardly disputable*, means to do *captation*. Latour explains this concept using a metaphor; captation is like building a dam. It would be absurd if the engineer who builds a dam thought that the water would take the course he or she intended, and was able to become overfilled without flooding. On the contrary, the engineer must assume that if there are leaks in the dam the water will go places he or she doesn't want it to. Similarly, if you leave the slightest chance of leak, the reader of the policy will move in unplanned directions (the next section is possible to see which bookkeeping system to use and how to do the depreciation). So what needs to be certain is if the player is free, that the dam is built deep enough. Because if the dam (in this case the policy) is built well, the reader will feel free to follow it. This metaphor suggests that *captation* is a technique used to make a policy less "questionable", as a consequence less subject to dispute. In this documentary analysis, the most striking aspect that reveals the lack of *captation* is the lack of clarity about the mandatory implementation of accrual accounting.

Thus from the first part of this analysis focused on the non-human actors, on the light of the logical text model, is evident how the construction of the decree since in its input stage is not approachable at what computer since is defined as a script. Indeed, there is not a linear list of commands able to drive the implementers in building the technology. As a consequence, the input stage of the policy is not placed next to a blueprint. From the beginning, there is a lack of consistency; specifically from the first draft of the Act 339, when the Ministry chooses to write that accrual accounting is an instrument for cognitive purposes. This decision was strongly criticized by academics (i.e., see comment prof. Pozzoli). The negative modalities shown in Fig. 4.5 are attributable to distorted ways of implementation that alienates the accrual accounting from a fact in its being constructed, and approaches to its being an artifact.

Thus, the questions to be answered in the next section are: If the policy is not a blueprint, can the player avoid implementing part of it? Is it possible to take other paths?

This aspect will be better shown in the next section, where are presented the initial result of implementation.

5.5 The Evaluation Path, Initial Results

Thus, after the content analysis of the input phase of the policy, we focus our attention on the analysis of the third stage, the evaluation of the output. We will analyze the translation phase more deeply through a micro-sociological study in a laboratory. On 28th of December 2011, a decree of Prime Minister defines a trial period for the reform implementation. The 1st of January 2012 officially starts the trial (lasting two years) as it relates to the implementation of new accounting systems and financial statements in the regions, local authorities, and their institutions. This trial aims to identify any critical components for the resulting changes, achieving a more effective regulation of this issue. The article 6 of the Decree:

> [The regions and local authorities referred in the article 3 to the start of the trial have to flank, for cognitive purposes, the accrual accounting to the cash accounting, ensuring the unique detection of the operational events both in terms financial and economic]... [**In order to allow the implementation of the accrual accounting** is referred to the regulation related to the updating of the inventories, which are the main source about the description and evaluation of the balance sheet] (Art 6 DPSM 28th December 2011).

Since the beginning of the trial, the Ministry and the institutional bodies responsible for monitoring of the trial have issued documents in which they provided feedback about the output of the reform. Typically, these documents contained a semestral evaluation period.

This is the report about the first year of trial (2012), from the Minister of Economy and finance, Saccomanni:

> [**The most of the bodies in the trial has elected to defer to 2013 the implementation of the accrual accounting**, chart of accounts and the consolidated financial statements .... A limited number of local governments have not availed itself of the option to postpone to 2013 this part of the accounting reform, have adjusted its accounting statements at the beginning n. 3 and adopting the integrated accounts. It is reasonable that these entities also will prepare the consolidated financial statements with their own group of companies (Ministro dell'Economia e delle Finanze Saccomanni, 23 maggio 2013)].

Then, during the first 6 months of 2013, in his report the Minister wrote:

> [*the Regions in the trial have indicated the need to deepen the Accrual Accounting Principle with particular referenceto* ***paragraphs 4.15 and 6.1****,concerning* ***the value of fixed assets****and the discipline* ***of depreciation***. Specifically, referring to the State property and to the assets that do not have an historical cost, the evaluation criteria were determined using, if possible, the Decree from Ministry of Economy and Finance of 18th of April, 2002 "New classification of assets and liabilities of the assets of the State and their criteria evaluation". The observations

- To consider the actor outside of the process, including the role of academics and consultants;
- To evaluate how the process in which they are involved and the object in construction is altered.

The large period of observations, 18 months of analysis, yielded a large body of data; considered the volume of material, it is not possible to report all the observations collected. Thus, only a fraction of which, where the accrual accounting issue is present, is used in the present research.

In his book "Laboratory life", Latour declares that "....conversations between practicing scientists provide a potentially fruitful source of data which has thus far been largely neglected in the studies of scientific practice (Latour & Woolgar, 1979, p. 166)". Latour also explains the motivations behind his assertion using a diagram, which is reported here. The diagram represents the different explanations of the conversation reported in the laboratory. In this diagram, Latour shows how facts are socially constructed.

As Latour suggests, "we started by identifying the different networks in which [accrual accounting] had meaning and by survey the area in which it was created". "We started by identifying the different networks in which accrual accounting had meaning and by surveying the area in which it was created. To look at the construction of accrual accounting is not simply to deny its solidity as a fact. Rather is to emphasize how, where and why it was created (Latour & Woolgar, 1979, p. 127)" (Fig. 6.2).

This figure further represents the theoretical guideline (along with those already described above) followed to analyze the video call conversations. Specifically is observed:

- *who* made the *inscriptions*, the main actors involved;
- *what* was argued during that meeting;
- *how* the arguments were written and published in the final version of the policy.

Indicating the name of participant in the dialogue was not permitted because others responsible for the trial, from other regions, also took part in each conversation. However, we did specify the role of the actors involved in the conversation, referring to the circle of institutional players involved in the conversations including the individual's *profession*, for example, academics, consultants from the National Association of Accountants, and the employees of the entities.

Then we show what these players argued in terms of different proposals. During these conferences, distinctive topics were discussed, including the entire background of the implementation project, accounting principles, comments from government committees, and information and technology gaps. Key issues related to the accrual accounting that players discussed included depreciation and the evaluation of historical assets and accrual and liquidity concepts, among others.

Latour says, "....a major obstacle to the study of thought processes is the absence of written records (Latour & Woolgar, 1979, p. 168)". Fortunately, in this case, a range of documents relevant to the daily activities of the laboratory were collected. These included drafts and reports of video call conversations. Indeed, at the end

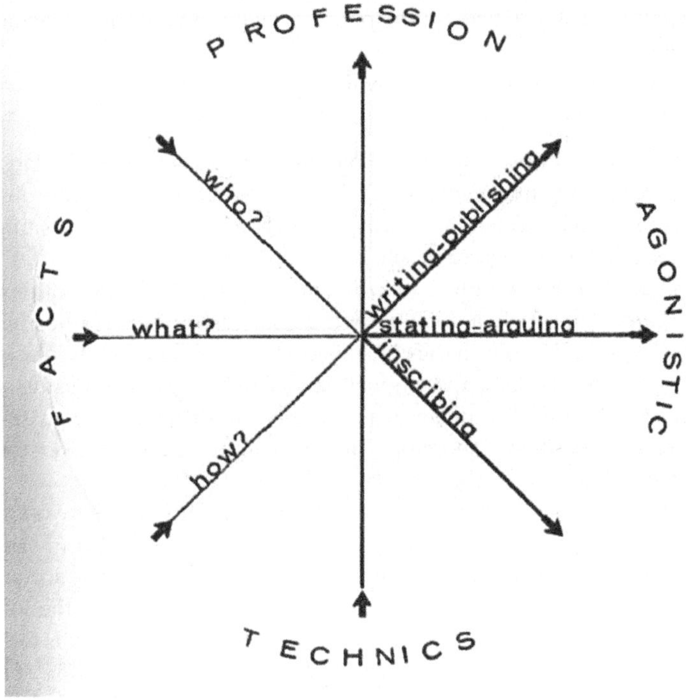

Fig. 6.2 The microprocessing of facts. *Source* Original figure from Latour, "Laboratory life" page 167

of the discussion, a "working draft" was prepared; this report was an inscription (discussion notes), which provided us with a useful opportunity to closely analyze the construction of facts. In the table, we summarize some parts of the dialogue from the video call conversation about the interpretations and fabrications related to accrual accounting implementation.

6.2 The Analysis of Literary Inscriptions

Latour says that the laboratory objects are accomplished by the imposition of *several documents* obtained from inscription devices within the laboratory or *from papers by investigators outside the laboratory* (Latour & Woolgar, 1979, p. 84). "The laboratory activity is a constant struggle for the generation of and acceptance of particular type of statement" (Latour & Woolgar, 1979, p. 81). "A laboratory is constantly performing operations on statements; adding modalities, citing, enhancing, diminishing, borrowing and proposing new combinations. Each of these operations can result in a *statement*, which is either different or qualified qualification of existing facts. Each statement, in turn, provides the focus for similar operations in other laboratories. Members of our laboratory regularly noticed how assertions were rejected, borrowed, quoted, ignored, confirmed, or dissolved. Some laboratories frequently manipulated of statements while elsewhere there was thought to be little activity" (Latour & Woolgar, 1979, pp. 86–87).

Thus, following Latour's theory, the work of the laboratory can be understood in terms of the continual generation of a variety of documents. These documents result from the transformation of statements from their *fact-like status*. This kind of activity is called the *literary inscription*. This is the *microprocess of fact construction in science*. It depends on the writing and reading process. In other words, it depends on *literary inscription*.

Latour asserts that "the function of literary inscription is the successful persuasion of readers" (Latour & Woolgar, 1979, p. 76); however, as underlined in the previous chapter, "the readers are only *fully convinced* when all sources of persuasion seem to have disappeared…There is, then, an essential *congruence between a fact* and the *successful operation of various process of literary inscription.* A text or statement can be read as fact when readers are sufficiently convinced that there is no debate about…" (Latour & Woolgar, 1979, p. 76). Thus, literary inscription is of central importance in laboratory activity. In this section, this process is examined by looking at reports involving transcribed conversations and discussions between members of the laboratory.

"The literary inscription is a five-fold classificatory scheme corresponding to different types of statements" (Latour & Woolgar, 1979, p. 76); in other words, it is a sequence of typologies of statements that explain the gradual passage from the *statement as fact* to the *statement as artifact* (Fig. 6.3).

The typical epistemological approach is followed in Fig. 6.3 It starts from the first step, in which it is possible to find statement type 5 corresponding to a *taken for granted fact*, "*things that everybody knew* (Latour & Woolgar, 1979, p. 76)". Latour says, "precisely, because they were taken for granted, our observer found that such statements rarely featured in discussions between laboratories (Latour & Woolgar, 1979, p. 76)". Continuing with the figure, the *statement type 4* formed

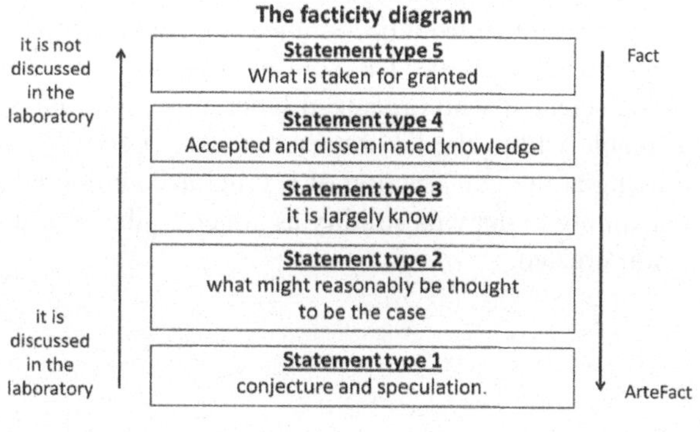

Fig. 6.3 The facticity diagram

part of the *accepted knowledge disseminated for example* through teaching text. In general, Latour says that scientific textboxes contain a large number of sentence type 4.

In the middle of the path is *statement type 3*, which includes what "*is largely known*". An example is "The structure of GH.RH was reported to be X", which is not the same to say "GH.RH is X". In other words, "A is in relationship with B" but there are *circumstances affecting the basic relationship*, external variables, which affect the statement. This includes the aspect that has been established as general practice over the years.

Looking at the base of the pyramid are *statements type 2*, which indicate "*what might reasonably be thought to be the case*". It is clear how this is closer to claim than fact. It is more like a suggestion. Finally, there are *statements type 1*, which comprise conjecture and speculation.

In this research, the object observed in the laboratory is the accrual accounting. The analysis will be made through the documents produced in the laboratory by internal actors involved in its implementation and the papers sent by external actors, as academics, who are outside the laboratory. This research will present data from "laboratory as a system of literary inscription (Latour & Woolgar, 1979, p. 105)". Specifically, during the analysis of our discussions, we will examine the parts related to the accrual accounting, differentiating between the issues that are not the subject of discussion (type 5), because it has been accepted, known, and taken for granted (we will see that there are very few because it questioned almost the entire accounting system). Then, we will highlight *type 4* statements related to the accrual accounting, which are mainly the actions undertaken by academics. Finally, more frequent will be statements *type 3, type 2, and type 1*, which contain all the statements, the guesses on accrual accounting. Specifically, statements of *type 3* are all the beliefs and bad habits hinged on those public entities that have tried to implement accrual accounting systems in the past.

Statements *type 2* and *type 1* are related to the completely unknown issues, areas of difficulty when it comes to implementation. At the same time, there is an ample opportunity for manipulation among them. For example, this might involve the depreciation or the choice of scriptural system of double entry. We will demonstrate the frequency of *statement type 3, type 2, and type 1.* The solidity of accrual accounting, which prevents it from becoming a subjective artifact, is created by the steady accumulation of technique. This solidity depends on the "laboratory routine, the iron hand of the scientist who organized laboratory work and took all necessary precautions available within the laboratory context" (Latour & Woolgar, 1979, p. 127). Thus, looking at the construction of accrual accounting adopting a critical perspective is not simply to deny its solidity as a fact. Rather, it emphasizes how, where, and why it was created.

6.3 The First Step of Emergence of Accrual Accounting

In November 2011, the President of Campania Region, in an anticipated Decree (Regional Decree n. 255 on November 15, 2011) initiated a workgroup (four employers in the accounting sector responsible for the trial), to implement and shape the new reform. Thus, following the timeline, from the second semester of 2012 (June–December) and for all of 2013, we will report the abstract of the conversations where accrual accounting issues are discussed. Indeed, through the summary of these observations, we will reconstruct the complex "*technological structure*" activated in the entities to enable the implementation of accrual accounting. Specifically, the analysis shows the contributions of the technicians, consultants, and academics who theorize, motivate, promote, or disapprove the fabrication of accrual accounting.

5th of June 2012: Consultants from the National Association of Accountants took part in this conference. Specifically, they addressed two topics: one is purely related to bookkeeping records and the other one concerns *the adoption of IPSAS*. The consultants observed that: "the current principles approved by decree are based *on different criteria* from those established by IPSAS. For example, there is a difference regarding the depreciation of land. In the Italian policy there is no depreciation of land" (Report Gruppo di Lavoro, 5/06/2012, p. 1).

In general, the land has an unlimited useful life and should not be written off (Paragraph 4.15, Annex n. 3). In the IPSAS, there is depreciation. In consideration of these discrepancies, the group *asked the Minister directly to express a formal opinion on the adoption of IPSAS*.

The accountants in the group work also prepared an example of the method of bookkeeping records *of fixed assets*. Specifically, this focused on *the depreciation*, and the investment grants, specifically the *adjustment entries*. There is no specified way to record depreciation. During debates, they discussed two possibilities for recording depreciation: First to do the deduction directly based on the value of the property, and second to use the account "Accumulated Depreciation". They opted for the direct deduction of the value of the asset instead of using the enhancement of accumulated depreciation. They adopted the *direct method*, which is to detect and curtail the depreciation on the value of the asset, without using the account "Accumulated Depreciation" or "Depreciation Fund". That account is not present in the schema of the balance sheet. This was the consultants' decision. However, in spite of this decision, those responsible for trials confirm that doubt about this decision remains. "If the detection of accumulated depreciation is present in the financial accounting is it ensured the perfect reconciliation between two systems and two results (accrual and financial)?" This question will remain unresolved.

The group also decided to adopt the deferred income regarding bookkeeping records of government grants related to investment for the purchase of fixed assets. This was decided due to the multi-annuality transaction. By handling this issue using this method, it is possible to suspend the contribution of shares in the financial years in which they are paid by the lender in adjustment entries.

26th of June 2012: During this conference, those responsible for trial discussed the definition of the *state of completion of work in economy*. However, "this issue appears too difficult to resolve without the consultants from the National Association of Accountants, so the group decided to postpone the issue to the next conference (Report gruppo di lavoro, 26/06/2012, p. 1)". In addition, video conference participants discussed *Memorandum accounts*[1] and *Clearance accounts*,[2] because the difference between them is not evident from the policy document. The National Standard Code for company specifies that memorandum accounts be recorded once (Standard n. 22). The National Standards about the memorandum accounts are also analyzed; however, the difference is not yet clear, and it was decided to request further clarification from the Consultant of the National Association of Accountants. However, they asked also a clarification from academic *consultant* (Professor Mussari) about this issue. In his report, he specifies: "…the similarities are only apparent and deceptive. Entries recorded in the memorandum accounts are placed at the foot of the balance sheet, i.e. outside of it, and do not participate in any way in the determination of net assets. On the contrary, clearance accounts are part of the budgetary system. They (as memorandum accounts) do not affect the final recorded result because in circumstances when recourse to such accounts is made by the government, there is a contra entry, with both debit and credit for the same amount in respect of third parties" (Mussari, 2012, p. 2).

10th of July 2012: During this video conference, the group discusses topics related to the video call conference of 5th of June, including how to do the records of depreciation. In a striking move, they decided to adopt a solution opposite to the one agreed on prior. Instead of using the direct mode to reflect depreciation of the building, The National Standard Code (OIC) expects to be done with indirect mode, which is using the Depreciation Fund. The main reason for the decision is to provide greater transparency. At this point, it is likely the group will "adopt the indirect method and maybe it's even easier for the public entities (Report gruppo di lavoro, 10/07/2012)".

During this video conference, they also give a further definition of the *state of completion of work in economy* by analyzing a complex example, which sets forth *a simulation of recording*. This simulation, *as internally developed*, *represents an integration of the principle of accrual accounting*. The example is read, discussed, and also integrated with the bookkeeping records about the building process, including those specified for the transfer of monetary contribution from other entities (grant). Some questions are as follows: "Is an asset in the financial statement when it is acquired and available and not just when is part of the property?" "Is the liquidity time

[1]Memorandum accounts are utilized to note information about the funds to be due to be paid to, or received from other organizations; these records are for information purposes only. www.reverso.net.

[2]Clearance accounts are temporary accounts which hold costs until they can be transferred elsewhere. For example, a company might use a clearing account to hold revenue and costs when completing year-end fiscal calculations. When the company has finished placing the revenue and costs in the account, it can then transfer the amount to the company's net earnings. www.reverso.net

different from the time of the payment order?(Report gruppo di lavoro, 10/07/2012, p. 2)". This is a clear example of missing staging and framing in the policy, which forced the actors to create it.

17th of July 2012: The group confirms the decision to proceed with the indirect depreciation method. As a consequence, they ask the Minister to integrate the Chart of Accounts, adding the "Depreciation Fund".

27th of July 2012: This represents the last meeting before a brief interruption (summer break). Those responsible for trial perform a final overview of the first year of trial, evaluating *the opportunity to postpone the implementation of accrual accounting for 1 year* for two main reasons:

- "first of all because it is devoting more effort to the implementation of a revised version of the traditional commitment and cash accounting,
- second because there is not *a pre-built packages* for the system" (Report gruppo di lavoro, 27/07/2012). For example, the construction process for a new technologic informative system hasn't begun. Specifically, this request will be advanced to the Ministry in September and will be emphasized that it is a specific request from the regions, the level of government without previous experience in this field.

Here, they anticipated a problem related to the evaluation of assets. Indeed, one participant notes that there is potential for *incorrect evaluation of assets*, specifically the heritage assets. The solution suggested in the conversations is the request for external (expertise). However, all the responsible individuals agree that this solution is too expensive to realize. The group will resume the discussion in September after further investigation.

22nd of October 2012: The group revisits the topic addressed at the last meeting on 10th of July, the *simulation of recording* of *a capital grants* to other entities, aimed at the acquisition of fixed assets. The main problem is "it is hard to collect data at the government recipients' contribution for the year in which the work is completed and then the moment by which start the depreciation of assets built" (Report gruppo di lavoro, 22/10/2012).

30th of October 2012: "The state of completion of work is a hard criteria to follow (Report Gruppo di Lavoro, 30/10/2012, p. 2)"; thus, they request to change the accrual basis of accounting again; about the possibility of change the text of the policy, expecting to receive a negative response from the Minister, "*it is agreed to proceed* from now to the *preparation of an amendment* to be proposed when the co-ordination will have to express opinion about the amendment of the policy" (Report Gruppo di Lavoro, 30/10/2012, p. 2). Specifically, it provides a simplification: considering that the assets financed by capital grants are not included in the assets of the region, the proposal suggests that contributions be recorded in the income statement in the year in which the payment is made. The group agrees with this interpretation.

In the same meeting, the group also discusses renaming the *provision for bad debts;* "there is the need of 'split' the provision to the fund risk, recorded in profit and loss account (accrual accounting), and *the bad debt provision*,[3] recorded in balance sheet (financial accounting). By removing the link it is necessary to *modify the accrual basis of accounting" (*Report gruppo di lavoro, 30/10/2012). The participants are invited to make quick proposals and define a new name.

On 5th of November 2012, the working group of the Minister accepts the request to simplify the principle from Regions; "thus it will be modified also accordingly to the example (simulation) attached (Report gruppo di lavoro, 5/11/2012)". Then, on 12th of November 2012: regarding the recording of capital grants to other entities finalized to the construction of fixed assets, the *individuation of the cost*, the group decides to "link the cost to *the moment of liquidation of the work*" (Report gruppo di lavoro, 12/11/2012), in other words, with reference to the progression of the building work. So this is the main change concerning the *definition of accrual basis of accounting*.

30th of November 2012: The National Union of Provinces (which are an intermediate level of government between regional and local governments) also takes part in this meeting. In the document about capital grants aimed at the realization of works that confirm the match between the cost to the liquidation time, it was noted that, on a practical level, "this method of accounting would make it impossible to finance by debt capital grants" (Report gruppo di lavoro, 30/11/2012). Considering that the State finances, for the most part, are financed by debt, it is evident how is tricky to translate private accounting into the public sector without appropriate adjustments.

On 3rd of December 2012, taking the observations made in the previous video conference call regarding the definition and records *of cost* in the income statement, a new hypothesis is designed to link *cost with the commitment*. However, some express concerns because "***this moves away from the concept cost known in the private sector***" (Report gruppo di lavoro, 3/12/2012). Another complex element is also introduced; what happens if the event contributions are withdrawn? This case is not explained in the simulation.

10th of December 2012: The policy is integrated with the interpretations about two issues discussed during 2012, *depreciation* and *memorandum accounts*. Other issues will be discussed during 2013 including the unresolved issue of evaluating heritage assets. During this meeting, all the integrations that are made to the accrual accounting principle contained in the policy are clarified. First of all, "the principle is integrated with all the examples conveyed about the accounting entries of the investment grants for the construction of fixed assets. Then the principle is integrated as it relates to memorandum accounts, adopting the note sent by prof. Mussari" (Report gruppo di lavoro, 10/12/2012). What remains unclear because due to the confused text of the decree is the *evaluation of particular assets*, such as.

[3]The provision for bad debts might refer to the balance sheet account also known as the Allowance for Bad Debts, Allowance for Doubtful Accounts, or Allowance for Uncollectible Accounts. In this case, Provision for Bad Debts is a contra asset account (an asset account with a credit balance). It is used along with the account Accounts Receivable in order to report the net realizable value of the accounts receivable. Source: https://www.accountingcoach.com/.

• *assets* in which *there is not an estimation of the historical value;*
• *assets* which have been *fully depreciated*;
• *assets* included in the *state property* and transferred by the State for *which there is not an estimate of the value.*

Therefore, ***the evaluation criterion*** that forms the basis of **the principle is not clear**. Indeed, to estimate the value of these assets, the entities should rely on the expertise of consultants in these areas. However, "there would be to sustain exorbitant costs (Report gruppo di lavoro, 10/12/2012)"; thus, participants wonder if there is a means to predict *simplified criteria of evaluation* for these categories of assets.

6.4 Some Stories of Doubts

In this collection of observations, it is clear that the accrual accounting system was not built systematically but is the product of a "heterogeneous engineering" (Gherardi & Lippi, 2000, p. 125) that starts from a series of partial contributions due to the inaccurate policy content. Moreover, it is clear that in fabrication processes there are no precise and formal rules to follow; therefore, human and non-human actors form a jumble.

After this brief chronological narrative, we will outline the characteristics of the different artifacts, trying to reconstruct their origin, the technical features, the evolution paths, and their relationship with human factors. These are the main arguments addressed during the semester June-December 2012 which are summarized in the table. In the semester June-December 2012, the possible **adoption of IPSAS** is the subject of one discussion. So in terms of frequency and priority, it is possible to confirm that poor attention is paid to this issue. Indeed, the consultants pointed out that the principles contained in the policy are far from the IPSAS framework but are strongly linked to the national accounting standards for company (OIC). Since this is a reform which aims to harmonize public sector accounting, this aspect is worthy of attention because it seems to be a missed opportunity (Table 6.1).

In the next table are summarized the empirical dimensions **about the Depreciation** (Table 6.2).

Table 6.1 Empirical dimensions of fabrication on the adoption of IPSAS

Observation	WHAT Initial accrual accounting elements	WHO Key actors involved	HOW Mechanisms of construction in accrual accounting
05/06/2012	Adoption of IPSAS	Technicians and Consultant of the National Associations of Accountants	The consultant observed that the current principles approved by decree are based on different criteria than those established by IPSASB

Table 6.2 Empirical dimensions of fabrication on the Depreciation

Observation	WHAT Initial accrual accounting elements	WHO Key actors involved	HOW Mechanisms of construction in accrual accounting
05/06/2012	Depreciation	Technicians and Consultant of the National Associations of Accountants	Depreciation of assets: There is agreement to detect the operating cost directly to deduction of the value of the asset
10/07/2012	Depreciation	Responsible for trial of each region. Consultant of National Associations of Accounts	Depreciation: During the last conversation, they agree to use the procedure into account. However, the Consultants of National Associations of Accounts don't agree. They suggest to use the accumulated depreciation
17/07/2012	Depreciation	Technicians	On the 05th of June the responsible of trial decides to build the bookkeeping record (in count); on the contrary, in this discussion was decided to use the accumulated depreciation account and for that reason the chart of accounts is modified
27/07/2012	The evaluation of assets	Technicians	There are potentially incorrect evaluations of assets; specifically, the heritage assets

On the issue of depreciation, the technical institutions are guided by the decision first taken, then denied, and then reconfirmed of consultants to adopt the indirect method for depreciation. Their strength of conviction, combined with the complete lack of knowledge of technicians, reaches the *integration of the policy* in the section of the chart of accounts.

At this point in the process, there is still much debate about how to handle the issue of depreciation. The group focuses on whether or not to recognize depreciation, for what types of assets, and using which evaluation method, among points.

The next table summarizes the different interpretations and machinations of the *accrual basis of accounting* (Table 6.3).

Starting from the discussion about a practical case, such as the records of capital grants aimed at acquisition or construction of building (a typical operation from Regions to other entities), it is clear how the *cost concept* is difficult to detect.

Table 6.3 The empirical dimensions of fabrication on the accrual basis of accounting

Observation	WHAT Initial accrual accounting elements	WHO Key actors involved	HOW Mechanisms of construction in accrual accounting
10/07/2012	Accrual basis of accounting: recording cost	Technicians	A further definition of accrual basis of accounting regarding the cost in the state of completion of work in economy.The resolution of these meeting will be part of the new version of the accrual basis of accounting standard
22/10/2012	Accrual basis of accounting: recording cost	Technicians	The state of completion of work is criteria hard to follow. It is requested to change the accrual basis of accounting
30/10/2012	Accrual basis of accounting: recording cost	Technicians	Preparation of an amendment about the amendment of the policy
05/11/2012	Accrual basis of accounting: recording cost	Technicians	The Minister has accepted the request of simplification of the principle from regions
12/11/2012	Accrual basis of accounting: recording cost	Technicians and Ministry of Economy and finance.	In the accrual basis of accounting, the cost is linked with the liquidation time in state of completion of work
30/11/2012	Accrual basis of accounting: recording cost	Technicians and Union of national provinces	It is noted that the cost = the liquidation time it is far from accrual accounting; thus, the standard from private sector cannot be transferred to the public without appropriate adjustments
03/12/2012	Accrual basis of accounting: recording cost	Technicians	A new hypothesis is to link **the cost= the commitment**

One vexing challenge is detecting the moment in which the cost rises. The decision becomes whether to link the cost to the commitment and preserves the tradition of the commitment accounting, or switching on the liquidation time, following a cash paradigm. The interpretation of the accrual basis of accounting is the core of the fabrication of accrual accounting construction. Often, artifacts are purely accounting

Table 6.4 Empirical dimension of fabrication on book-keeping technicalities

Observation	WHAT Initial accrual accounting elements	WHO Key actors involved	HOW Mechanisms of construction in accrual accounting
05/06/2012	Deferred income	Technicians	To adopt the deferred incomer recording the government grants
26/06/2012	Memorandum accounts	Technicians and Academic Consultant (Professor Riccardo Mussari)	There is no clarity in the policy about the difference between Memorandum accounts as Clearance accounts. The Academic specify the difference sending a note
30/10/2012	Bad debt provision	Technicians	Renaming the provision for bad debts modifying the accrual basis of accounting

and bookkeeping issues that demonstrate how rigid the technicians are and their fear of being manipulated. This aspect should not be overlooked because it demonstrates the concern of technicians of everyday life that will be carried out when accrual accounting is implemented. The lack of training, technical knowledge, and the doubts about the adoption of double-entry method create many practical issues (Table 6.4).

Many deviations from the implementation of accrual accounting are also related to *two non-human actors*: *the traditional budgetary accounting* and *the information and technology system* (Table 6.5).

Human actors as consultants aren't the only factors influencing this process. There are non-human actors that also play a role in this *rugby game*. The decision to postpone accrual accounting implementation is a clear signal of technicians' deviation. They are unable to achieve the result in the required time frame.

6.5 Accrual Accounting Implementation: New Stories

In this section, we will present the video conference call analysis from January 2013 to June 2013 (second semester of observation). Following the same method used in the previous section, we will be presenting the observations in chronological order, as the information was collected. These represent the reports on the weekly video conference (meeting) between experimenters. This is the diary that is compiled in the laboratory when scientists gather to perform experiments. Following that review is a schematization of the main artifacts of asset accounting designed to highlight the fabrications it has undergone.

Table 6.5 Empirical dimensions of stalled implementation

Observation	WHAT Initial accrual accounting elements	WHO Key actors involved	HOW Mechanisms of construction in accrual accounting
27/07/2012	Postpone the implementation of accrual accounting.	Technicians	The responsible of trial decides to ask the Ministry of Economy and finance to postpone the implementation of accrual accounting because there are many problems
10/12/2012	Rewriting the the accrual basis of accounting	Technicians and Ministry of Economy and finance	The policy **is integrated with the interpretations** about two issues discussed during 2012: about depreciation and **memorandum accounts.** Other issues will be discussed during the 2013 because remains **not resolved as the evaluation of heritage assets**

14 January 2013: During this conference, the technicians of the State Property and Heritage Assets Department of the Campania Region are invited to participate. Among the issues discussed is a shared ocument drawn up by the Regions involved in the trial. It aims to simplify the definition of the balance sheet, with particular reference to the case in which there are no elements to *evaluate assets*, because it is not possible to trace the value of the property for reasons of cost and/or time (for example, the appraisal carried out) (Report gruppo di lavoro, 14/01/2013, p. 1). This document, entitled "*Research material about fixed assets recording*" (*Approfondimenti su contabilizzazione delle immobilizzazioni materiali*), is sent to Professor Mussari, who also contributes comments. The attachment number 3 on the "Accrual Accounting Standard", in the Sects. 4.15 and 6.1, defines the guideline for accounting records, respectively, about depreciation (thus also on the Net Income Statement) and the evaluation of fixed assets (thus also on the balance sheet). The principle explicitly refers to the rules of the Civil Code and the National Accounting Standards established by the National Accounting Standards Board (OIC), specifically.

- Standard number 16 (OIC 16): fixed tangible assets;
- Standard number 24 (OIC 24): intangible assets.

The regions perceived many complexities related to the application of these accounting standards. For this reason, they will have a lengthy discussion about this issue. They also ask prof. Riccardo Mussari to provide some clarifications. The main problematic aspects are related to.

1. The absence of historical value of the acquisition;
2. The non-depreciation of land;
3. The differences between the state property and other buildings, specifically in terms of depreciation rates;
4. The evaluation of heritage assets.

Regarding *the historical value of acquisition*, as specified in section 6.1.2. of the attachment 3 the accrual basis of accounting standard, the "Tangible Assets should be recorded using the cost value of acquisition or the production value if made in economy (…), to net the depreciation (Allegato 3 DPCM 28 dicembre 2011, 2011, p. 13)". Thus, this is the principle established to choose the cost. However, the regions face difficulties when reconstructing the historical value of the assets property. Specifically, a group of technicians in one region stated that this information is absent in the majority of cases. In other cases, it cannot be reconstructed, for example, in the case of the beaches. At this point, the *machination process* of problem-solving that will lead to policy change begins. This is a formal aspect, and to the *fabrication of accrual accounting* as substantial aspect. A first solution to the problem, suggested by the Technicians of the State Property Department, is provided by an *independent expert, an evaluation report*. However, this solution does not appear viable to the Technicians Accounting Department, for two main reasons:

- There are significant costs to seek this expertise.
- Wherever determined, this value would have a current value. It is far from the cost method. In addition, there would be assets evaluated using the historical cost method, and other evaluated using the replacement cost method;
- It is anticipated also that if this solution is adopted, it will have an impact on *depreciation* which is defined in section 4.1.5. of the attachment 3 *the accrual basis of accounting standard*, "Depreciation begins when the asset is ready for use, i.e. when it is in the location and in the condition necessary for it to work as expected by the Entity. (Allegato 3 DPCM 28 dicembre 2011, p. 6)". If the depreciation starts from the time of appraisal, it would not adhere to this principle.

Considering the disagreements between the technicians, a single solution was proposed and accepted "*the exclusion of these assets from the presentation in the balance sheet*" (Report gruppo di lavoro, 14/01/2013, p. 3). The group also decided to add an Annex to the balance sheet, a list of assets including qualitative and quantitative information on such goods. If these items were sold, this would provide evidence of the transactions in the accrual accounting system and in the balance sheet as a traditional sell. The answer by the Ministry responded to that solution by stating: "*it is considered not possible to exclude the State property assets from the Balance Sheet*; considered the problematic aspect related to the evaluation it was agreed the request for further investigations" (Report gruppo di lavoro, 14/01/2013, p. 6). This is a clear example of *not linear translation* and the *distortion of the policy* not to present the assets in the balance sheet.

Regarding the principle of non-depreciation of land in Sect. 4.15 of Appendix 3, it specified that "In general, land has an unlimited useful life and should not be depreciated (Allegato 3 DPCM 28 dicembre 2011, p. 6)". The Minister is asked to confirm this statement, and the group also considers the observations made previously by accountants about the distance dictated by IPSAS. This principle is confirmed. The same Sect. 4.15 of Appendix 3 shows the *depreciation rates for state property assets* and the *depreciation rate for other buildings*; in particular, the statement specifies that buildings have a fixed depreciation *rate of 2%* and a depreciation period of 50 years. For *state property* assets, the depreciation rate *is 3%*. The reason for the two different rates is not clear, especially considering the goods are quite similar and perform the same functions. After several arguments about it, *is the* group decides *that even state property assets should have a 2% depreciation rate*. It's clear that once again, the text was written without avoiding attacks, and there is a new change addressing the issue of heritage assets by accountants and technicians of the State Property Department.

Specifically, it notes that "the Sect. 6.1.2 of Appendix 3 does not clarify a few things:

- What accounting treatment should be provided for heritage assets (assets or otherwise) for which it is not possible to determine a monetary value?
- For goods of historical and cultural values, the principle of non-depreciation is enshrined. However, how should goods that have cultural value as historical palaces or art but serve a purpose as any other building (for example are used as a venue for offices with regular leases) be treated?" (Report gruppo di lavoro, 14/01/2013, p. 6). These questions are very delicate and are necessary to deeply understand and discuss also in successive meetings (Report gruppo di lavoro, 14/01/2013, p. 6).

During this video conference, the technicians dictated the criteria aimed at preparing the first balance sheet. Thus, they draw a first balance sheet structure that is the result of the machinations that have given so far.

(a) "Assets and land: will be recognized at acquisition cost and if not available at the cadastral value (Report gruppo di lavoro, 14/01/2013, p. 6)". In the previous conference call, the group decided to determine the *depreciation accumulated fund*, considering the initial moment in which the asset has begun to be used and the average useful life of the type of asset. This has to be deducted from the asset value and is therefore a net asset value.

(b) "The properties of third parties available and used by the entities should be evaluated at acquisition cost, if not available at the cadastral value. This value is recorded in the memorandum accounts" (Report gruppo di lavoro, 14/01/2013, p. 6).

    (a) Books (Library): For this property, it is necessary to use an inventory survey. For these goods, a purchase cost should be identified as should the accumulated depreciation. If contributions from third parties aimed at the acquisition of books are received, it has been recorded in "Accrued expenses and deferred income and investment grants.

(b) Loans.
(c) Capital contributions, which are any contributions received for the financing of fixed assets, should be included in Accrued and Deferred investment grants". This issue was discussed many times during the first semester, including a discussion on how to record capital grants aimed at acquiring or constructing building (Table 5.3).
(d) Financial assets that are evaluated using the value of the acquisition. Investments are accounted for using the equity method.
(e) Cash and cash equivalents, all of the amounts in bank accounts.
(f) Surplus (Residual income) and liabilities (Residual expenses) are attributable to credits and debts, fund for risks and charges, and other funds.
(g) Debts and credits for taxations;
(h) Financial liabilities; long-term loans;
(i) Surplus from previous financial year;
(j) Endowment Fund of the entity: difference between assets and liabilities.

The balance sheet must be accompanied by a specific explanatory note describing in detail the evaluation methods adopted for assets and liabilities.

21st of January 2013: Regarding the proposal related to the first balance sheet preparation criteria, the working group asked to investigate the following aspects:

- "For the determination of the cadastral value of a property, for which there is no historical value of 'acquisition', it asks for confirmation that this value is the one obtained by the application of suitable *parameters and multiplying the cadastral income* (property). If confirmed it then becomes necessary to establish a shared and unique version of these parameters and multipliers (for example, those provided by the tax laws)(Report gruppo di lavoro, 21/01/2013, p. 1)".
- "*Endowment fund* for the institution. The working group considers it necessary to further investigate *the mode of determination of these accounts* in order to prevent any problems that may arise from the systematic calculation of the difference between the total assets and the total liabilities in the balance sheet. It is vital also to clarify *the meaning* of this item in the first balance sheet of the entity and the rules that determine its evolution (possible positive and negative variations) in subsequent years in relation to the events management" (Report gruppo di lavoro, 21/01/2013, p. 1).
- "Surplus: please to make in note that the item 'Operating results of previous years' *is not covered in the items of the chart of accounts.* In addition, *is not clear why these items were inserted* since it is a typical account from commitment and cash accounting system, not accrual accounting" (Report gruppo di lavoro, 21/01/2013, p. 1).

25th of February 2013: One of the issues discussed on this date was again about the evaluation of historical assets because there is still no clarity on the issue. In the last conference, those responsible for each regional trial decided to suggest the *non-inclusion of assets* in the balance sheet when the value was not available. The

Ministry rejected this solution. He suggested that the clarification refers to parameters and multipliers to the cadastra. However, the Ministry did not specify what kind of parameters should be used. Considering the importance of this issue, the group asked Prof. Mussari to clarify the issue. Prof. Mussari wrote a note and sent it to workgroup. They discussed it on the 4th of March 2013. He wrote that the arguments raised are very complex. It seems that the intention and purpose of having the entities escape the evaluation of assets, and the related procedure depreciation was to modify the balance sheet criteria to avoid constructions in order to simplify it. Thus, the objective of this draft is to provide an opinion about this possibility. He will focus first of all on the *evaluation issue* and then on the *depreciation.* Regarding the evaluation, he offered a historical reconstruction concerning the evaluation of the state property. Specifically, he states that "state property has always been subject to reporting (the law of 1964 'The law Curti' provided the depreciation for the state property), but this representation is never accurate because it was done on the basis of commitment and cash accounting (Mussari, 2013)". Regarding the assets of the Public entities, the professor clarified that we have basically two categories of goods:

- *state property*: roads, ports (heritage assets), buildings recognized for artistic, historical, archaeological, in accordance with the laws; collections of museums, galleries, archives, libraries. The main characteristic of the goods that are part of the public domain is their inalienable (Article 822 of the Civil Code).
- *non-state-owned assets*: for all other logical exclusion, defined simply as *assets.*

State property, both in doctrine and in practice, has always been considered as not evaluable because it cannot be sold to gain an appreciation in value. Specifically, in relation to the regions, the Art. 27 of Legislative Decree no. 76/2000 provides that "the general account of the assets include: assets and financial liabilities; goods and real estate property; all other assets and liabilities" (art.27 LD 76/200). There is no specification regarding the inclusion or exclusion of state property; therefore, the decision to exclude this proper has prevailed for years. According to Decree n. 77/1995 local authorities should recognize state property in the Assets as Heritage Assets. Prof. Mussari suggests the regions follow the approach taken by local authorities. So if the suggestion is to enroll them in the asset account as Heritage Assets, the question arises how officials should evaluate them.

The evaluation scheme expected in the law was

- the cost;
- the amount of the outstanding debt for goods already purchased by the entity.

However, for *local authorities*, this has *never been done* because the law stipulates that in order for an asset to be recognized is must be "susceptible to evaluation". Therefore, many agencies have stated that the *assets were not susceptible to evaluation.* Another problem was in addition to evaluation challenges that assets could be purchased or donated. The technicians of the Campania region stated that in its case, the region has donated many assets. Indeed, in this case, the evaluation is much more complicated because it is necessary to choose the estimated market value at the acquisition date and this value has to be estimated by an expert in public accounting, an academic. He adds that, attributing a value to a state property received as a donation, there is an increase in equity but there should be no impact on the income statement. However, this type of accounting procedure requires caution in the assessment because it involves subjectivity.

At this point, the technicians from the regions' object, because the costs for an expert assessment are very high. To resolve this problematic issue, professor Mussari reiterates a general principle underlying the accounting that is: "*the benefits to provide economic and financial information in doing the reporting must outweigh its costs; therefore is necessary to consider whether the benefits of providing information, in the case on state property, outweigh the costs. However, while the costs are monetarily measurable, the benefits are not, and also the costs arising from the non-production of accounting information*" (Mussari, 2013, p. 6).

"The biggest problem is related the assets that are already in the entity and should be evaluated based on the amount of the outstanding debt is still endangered (art 230, section 4, letter a Legislative Decree 77/1995). So if we consider just this provision for the assets in which there are is no loan involved because the asset was donated, we could not perform an evaluation. Therefore it would be excluded from the equity. If this principle were confirmed, says the academic, a large part of state property currently belonging to the regions would not be evaluated. We must critically question this issue" (Mussari, 2013, p. 7).

In his note, professor Mussari, regarding the Depreciation, focused attention on this: Considering two fixed and constant rates in the law for local government:

- *for buildings 3%*
- *for roads and other state property 2%.*

The Civil Code (the discipline for company) provides instead that the depreciation for tangible and intangible assets to be made in relation to the remaining useful life (article 2426). So according to the discipline for local government, "depreciation does not have to affect the useful life of the asset, since the rates are already fixed" (Mussari, 2013, p. 9)". This difference, which seems to be formal, shows how the logical framework is different in private sector and in the public sector.

At this point, the fundamental question that professor raises is the following: "Is it right to apply the procedure to the depreciation of state property?" This accounting procedure serves "to disappear assets" from the balance sheet. Indeed, it shows how many of the assets has been consumed and must be replaced. (The amount set aside)(Mussari, 2013, p. 11)". He continues by stating that "the goal of a public entity should instead be to keep these assets. It is possible to increase value for transfer to the next generation so that they will enjoy at least the same extent as those who preceded them (intergenerational equity) (Mussari, 2013, p. 11)". The *Accumulated depreciation* built on following straight temporal line can give us an idea about the age of the property but cannot tell us what the expected costs are for future maintenance and what the conditions are of the assets in operation. This means that its accounting function is not properly assessed. In other words, *the accumulated depreciation of a*

Table 6.6 The evaluation of assets: more empirical dimensions

Observation	WHAT Initial accrual accounting elements	WHO Key actors involved	HOW Mechanisms of construction in accrual accounting
14/01/2013	The evaluation of assets and the first balance sheet	Technicians of Assets and Property Department; National Associations o f Accountants	**Evaluations of assets** in which there are no elements for the evaluation of historical assets; the different solutions are: the value is obtained by the application of appropriate parameters and multipliers to the cadastra; evaluation by an external expert; non-inclusion. **The non-inclusion is what they prefer**
22/01/2013	The evaluation of assets and the first balance sheet	Technicians	The **evaluations of assets** is necessary to establish a shared and unique version of the parameters the cadastral income since are the main instrument of evaluation; The **Endowment fund** It is vital also to clarify the meaning and the mode of determination of this accounts; **Surplus** is not clear the reasons of insertion of this items
25/02/2013	The evaluation of assets: a draft from Ministry of Finance	Technicians; Ministry of Economy and finance	In the last conference, the responsible of trial decides to suggest: **non-inclusion** of assets in balance sheet when the value is not available. This solution is rejected by the Ministry. He clarifies to refer to parameters and **multipliers to the cadastra;** however, the Ministry did not specify what kind of parameters. **Thus, it** was requested a clarification to Prof. Mussari.

(continued)

Table 6.6 (continued)

Observation	WHAT Initial accrual accounting elements	WHO Key actors involved	HOW Mechanisms of construction in accrual accounting
4/03/2013	The evaluation of assets: a comment from an academic	Technicians; Ministry of Economy and finance; Academic	In his comment, he suggests an historical asset needs to be **"susceptible of evaluation"**. However, **the benefits** of economic and financial reporting must be greater than its costs. So, the point is: assess whether **the benefits of providing information** (in this case on state property) are greater than the costs, and this is an issue related to the **"interpretation"** because the benefits are—often—difficult to qua ntify

6.6 Some Stories of Creations: The Construction of a New Object

During the period from June to December 2013, the subjects of discussions during the video conference applications are related to double-entry records of daily management operations. Thus, in consideration of the looming December 2013 deadline for the preparation of the first balance sheet, and after the discussion on principles and criteria during 18 months, the group starts to create and fabricate double-entry recording. Specifically, on 2nd of July 2013 they discussed the correct imputation of the cost related to the purchase of goods and services. Moreover, they added the complication of a dispute that emerges with sellers, a situation when it becomes necessary to create extraordinary losses or a write-down of assets in the balance sheet, which reduces the debt. The other question concerns the correctness of accounting records relating staff salary payments. After numerous discussions and the presentation of various accounting aspects, the group decided to send all of these questions to the technical representatives of the Ministry of Economy and Finance (Report video conferenza, 2/07/2013).

The interesting thing to note during this period is the fact that during the video conference the group discussed presentations (slides) of some cases that illustrate the implementation of the accrual accounting. So it is possible to analyze primordial systems in action. For example, on 21st October 2013, the group reviews the case of

Table 6.7 Accrual accounting: machinations on accounts

Observation	WHAT Initial accrual accounting elements	WHO Key actors involved	HOW Mechanisms of construction in accrual accounting
11/03/2013	Accrual accounting: updating the principle	Technicians; Ministry of Economy and finance; Academic	In the updating version of the principle, the properties are recorded at purchase cost or applying to the cadastral value. The entities have the option to apply **depreciation rates** greater than those indicated in the table, in consideration of the useful life of the asset
18/03/2013	Provision for doubtful debts and the double-entry method of record	Technicians; representatives of Ministry of Economy and finance	**To provide a correlation** between the accounts through a financial commitment of expenditure in respect of the provision for doubtful debts in accrual accounting: **Disadvantages and Advantages.** To implement the double-entry method of record: disadvantages and advantages
26/03/2013	Provision for doubtful debts and the depreciation	Technicians; representatives of Ministry of Economy and finance	To **not provide correlation** (uncouple the funds) so it is **not mandatory** to create in the budgetary accounting on financial basis a provision which is made in the accrual accounting
07/05/2013	Provision for doubtful debts and the depreciation	Technicians; academic; consultants	The decision to eliminate the reference to single-entry record; The non-correlation between the provision for doubtful debts in budgetary accounting and in accrual accounting

the province of Florence. In order to examine the first output of this reform, without going into the merits and only in the case of example, we report the salient factors illustrated by the technician representatives of Ministry of Economy and Finance. The province of Florence had already implemented a sort of *accrual accounting system for cost centers*. They had created a chart of accounts dividing the accounts of an accrual nature and accounts of a financial nature. The accounts were divided according to the type of the input to which they were related. However, the systems were not related to one other.

The main feature of this reform was the integration between the two accounting types. In other words, the objective was to make one accounting record both in financial terms and in accrual terms. The facilitation and the control of this operation were guaranteed by one fact; the chart of accounts is structured by the Ministry and cannot be changed by individual entities. So the chart of accounts should be a correlation matrix. However, to implement the new system initially, the technicians of the provinces of Florence tried to translate the old chart of accounts to the new chart of accounts by identifying an entry for the new plan using each item in the old plan. In other words, the accounts of the accrual nature are the accounts for revenues and expenses. The accounts of a financial nature are assets and liabilities for the balance sheet. As a way of records, the province of Florence has chosen to implement the *double-entry bookkeeping*. When it comes to defining the *accrual date*, the moment chosen as relevant for the imputation of the costs in the accrual accounting system is the liquidation time of the expenses in the financial accounting.

By analyzing the key issues of the accrual accounting implementation in the province of Florence, the entity reveals some doubts (the title of some slides presented during the video conference is "doubts"). Among these doubts is *the provision allowance for doubtful accounts*.

By comparison, in the same video conference, the Ministry of Economy and Finance presents the case accrual accounting system implementation in the province of Rome. Even in this presentation, there are slides entitled "Difficulties". Among the challenges outlined is the problem of the memorandum accounts. In particular, they claim that the representation of the *memorandum accounts* cannot be reconciled with the need for evidence in the balance sheet.

29th October 2013: During this conference, the group focuses on a question that comes from a municipality, which is trying to implement accrual accounting. In particular, there were some issues related to adjustment entries and the treatment of deferred income. Specifically, the municipality offers two different kinds of records, claiming that the management operation in question can be recorded in two different ways.

The consultant from the Campania region (from KPMG), who participate in the meeting realizes that double-entry bookkeeping is wrong, because it is made, on the contrary, reversing the positions of the accounts. After a few minutes, even technicians from other regions made the same observation.

The consultant of KPMG gives his interpretation of the problem and guides the technicians in the understanding of the question. A conversation follows between the consultant and the executive of the Campania region. Specifically, the discussion concerns taxes for building permits. The recording should be double, because it is necessary to record the credit for taxations for permission to build. This would be a voice of "income", which must be suspended and charged the following year. The consultant from KPMG declares: "This is a *suspended entry*. Is it allocating a reserve that appears in the heading of Shareholders or is it a deferred liability?(Report di video conferenza, 29/10/2013, p. 2)" There is no clarity. This issue is very delicate, since this kind of credit is very common in local government. Therefore, the group expects that this question will evolve and be subject to interpretation from the consultant of the Ministry.

5th of November 2013: During this video conference, the discussion is again on tangible fixed assets and depreciation rates. In particular, it focuses on the inconsistency that institutions report. The paragraph 4.18 of Annex 3 of the principle of accrual accounting contains a table with the depreciation rates to apply to certain classes of assets. It is taken from the "national handbook of Principles and accounting rules" of 2008. However, this table does not match up in many aspects of the asset classes contained in the Chart of Accounts. The technicians collected all the discrepancies and proposed solutions in a table distinguishing between the items using typology of asset. There is also the response of the Ministry of Economy and Finance, which confirms in most of the cases the interpretation proposed.

This is the English translation of the table which is included in the report of the video conference translated into English. During the discussion, all the issues are analyzed and discussed. In particular, regarding the plant and equipment in which there is no agreement with the response provided by the Ministry. However, everything is confirmed (Table 6.8).

18th November 2013: During this video conference, we analyze the assumptions of the frequently used accounting treatment of a case of operation common in public institutions, the f*ree loan for use* or *commodatum*. The technicians start to create a hypothesis. Hypothesis number 1 is that the free loan for use transaction represents a transaction because it involves less revenue for the institution. For this reason, it is necessary to do the recording in both, financial and accrual accounting systems. In contrast, hypothesis number 2, the free loan for use, is not a transaction, so it does not reduce revenues and therefore should not be made in records in financial and accrual accounting. The transaction is recognized among the memorandum accounts. The technicians decide to accept hypothesis 2 for two reasons. The first is because it is difficult to record as less reduced revenues. The second is because the consultants confirm that this practice is consolidated in the private sector; specifically, this type of transaction is regulated by two national accounting standards for private sector (OIC 16 and OIC 22).

25th of November 2013: During this conference, the technicians discuss the articulation of capital reserves on the balance sheet. In particular, it is the group made a comparison between the principle for private sector, the national standard n. 28 (OIC 28) and the principle of accrual accounting for public sector (which is still in construction). Specifically, the consultants illustrate how *Equity* is composed, following the standard OIC 28. They try to translate the same composition for public sector. Specifically, standard n. 28 states that *Equity* is composed in this way, Corporation stock;

Table 6.8 Table from video conference of 5th of November 2013

Asset	Problem	Solution proposed by technicians	The Ministry
Means of transport by road	The categories of Chart of Accounts provided for means of road transport do not correspond to Attachment 3 "Accrual accounting". **The Chart of Accounts** distinguishes between civil means of transport and military means of transport. The **Attachment 3**, instead, distinguishes between means of road transport "light", "heavy", and "for specific use"	The interpretation is: this distinction (light/heavy/specific use) should remain just for management purpose since it finds no representation in the chart of accounts	The Ministry confirms
Means of transport in general	For the remaining categories of vehicles (both military and civilian), **the depreciation rate is indeterminate**	Will be chosen for each single case the depreciation rate to be applied	The Ministry confirms
Plant and equipment	The application of the same depreciation rate (period 20 years, rate 5%) for plant and equipment and equipment raises some concerns because the equipment provided to public entities tend to have a useful life of less than 20 years	They ask to apply for the equipment a rate which is comparable to the office machines (20%)	The chart of depreciation is intended to be redefined through a glossary of the chart
Assets	The attachment 3, par. 4.18 provides that for State property and Not State property the rate is 3%, while for all other assets should be applied the rate of 2%	They ask to confirm that the depreciation rate for the Non-State Property assets remains 3%	The Ministry confirms. However, it is possible to do further amendments

(continued)

Table 6.8 (continued)

Asset	Problem	Solution proposed by technicians	The Ministry
Heritage assets	The attachment 3 provides that the historical, artistic, and cultural assets are not subject to depreciation. This rule includes the precious materials as gold	This rule includes the precious materials as gold, which is not depreciated	The Ministry confirms and provides also the integration of principle
Books	It should be noted that the table with the depreciation rates of the Attachment 3, section. 4.18 provides that the Books are depreciated with a **ratio of 5%, for a period of 20 years.** However, in the same attachment 3 section 6.1.2, there is a "special case": books which are part of libraries must be depreciated over a maximum **period of 5 years, with a rate of 20%**	They ask to use the rate of 20% and 5 years	The Ministry confirms the correct application of the 20% for books in libraries.
Equipment and clothing	It is not finding any representation in a dedicated account	They ask to confirm that this category is "Other assets"	The Ministry confirms that this is the residual item "Other"

additional paid-in shares; reserves (revaluation, legal, and statutory); reserve for own shares; other reserves, indicated separately; profit (loss) brought forward; and profit (loss) for the year. According to the accrual accounting principle in the policy, the Public Equity is articulated as follows: endowment fund; reserves from profit or loss from previous years, from stock and from building permits; and result (positive or negative) for the year (Fig. 6.4).

Some group members raise doubts about the proposed composition, specifically asking: "What is the meaning of "Capital reserves"? What do we have to include into this account?" How is the endowment fund built? Probably we will have to put the total value of the asset! (Report video conferenza, 25/11/2013)". At some point in the discussion, the technicians of public entities give the following interpretations: the *Capital Reserves* is equal to the *investment grants* and the *endowment fund is equal* to the *current assets.* At this point, the consultants involved in the video conference

Fig. 6.4 A comparison between private and public equities

A) Equity	A) Equity
Corporation stock	I-Endowment Fund
II-Additional paid-in shares	II-Reserves
III-revaluation reserves	a) profit or loss from previous years
IV-Legal reserve	b) From Capital
V-Statutory reserves	c) From building permits
VI Reserve for own shares	III Result (positive or negative) for the year.
VII-Other reserves, indicated separately.	Total shareholders' equity.
VIII-Profit (loss) brought forward.	
IX-Profit (loss) for the year	

have to clarify that the *Capital Reserves are not investment grants* but represents the total assets at the beginning of the year and *that the endowment fund* represents an initial contribution, *as a stock capital* in a company, which arise in the first balance sheet (it can be incremented or decremented during years). This interpretation is not entirely welcomed by technicians because it causes this result: The assets that the entity has acquired through investment grants it is not represented in the endowment fund, because it is still unavailable. However, the Ministry accepts the proposal from private consultants.

17th December 2013: The Campania region is encountering difficulties in applying the criteria for allocating the *allowance for doubtful accounts*. The technicians say that "the accrual accounting principle specifies that the allowance for doubtful accounts is not recorded among the liability items of the balance sheet, but is deducted from the credits to which it relates". Regarding its construction, the entities must "identify the categories of entry allocated, which may result in doubtful credit are difficult to collect. The level of analysis is left to the individual entities (Report di video conferenza, 17/12/2013, p. 1)".

There is some difficulty in performing this calculation, and there is *no assurance* regarding the *reliability of this value*. Therefore, the group asks the Minister if it is possible to write the amount separately. The item will be shown in the balance sheet among the liabilities instead of deducted from the credits amount. The Minister authorizes the Campania Region to adopt this procedure, but only for the trial. Regarding the calculation, the Minister clarifies that there is *no correlation* between *credits* of accrual accounting, *residuals receivables* of budgetary accounting and the calculation of the allowance for doubtful debts. This clarification is made explicit in the accrual principle, integrating it in Sect. 4.20.

It is possible to summarize the observation of the semester June-December 2013 in Table 6.9.

In the analysis of video conferences from this semester the entities continues to discuss some of the issues that still remain unclear, such as the *evaluation* and *depreciation of assets*. They discuss some issues related to the preparation of the first balance sheet and focus on some accounts that create more doubts of interpretation as the *allowance for doubtful credits*. Then they made the choice to adopt double-entry

Table 6.9 Empirical dimensions of construction (semester June–December 2013)

Observation	WHAT Initial accrual accounting elements	WHO Key actors involved	HOW Mechanisms of construction in accrual accounting
02/07/2013	Bookkeeping technicalities: double-entry recording	Technicians	The creation and fabrication of double-entry recording: some doubts about the correctness of the accounting records
21/10/2013	Accrual accounting system in action: the case of provinces of Florence and provinces of Rome	Technicians; representatives of Ministry of Economy and finance	The unresolved difficulties: the provision for allowance for doubtful accounts and the memorandum accounts. The provinces give their interpretations
29/10/2013	Bookkeeping technicalities: double-entry recording	Technicians; KPMG consultant	Some issues related to the adjustment entries and the treatment of deferred income. The consultant gives his interpretation guiding the counselor
05/11/2013	Evaluation of asset and depreciation	Technicians; consultants; Ministry of Economy and finance	The agreement and disagreement on depreciation rate for each typology of assets
18/11/2013	Bookkeeping technicalities: memorandum accounts and free loan for use	Technicians; consultants	The free loan for use is regulated using the memorandum accounts as in private sector
25/11/2013	The first balance sheet: the equity	Technicians; consultants	Capital Reserves and Endowment fund: meaning and composition unclear
17/12/2013	The first balance sheet: the allowance for doubtful accounts	Technicians; Ministry of Economy and finance	There is no assurance regarding the reliability of this value so the Minister authorizes to record it separately in the balance sheet

bookkeeping, and as a consequence they try to draw some records. Specifically, it is clear that some forces (the consultants) play a strong role in sensitive issues, such as the equity. It is demonstrated that they are not just addressing technical problems; they are forcing the core of accrual accounting concepts (that are still struggling to be clarified). Finally, after a year of trial, it is possible to explore the outcome of the implementation of accrual accounting in some *test cases* (Rome, Florence) that the representatives of the Ministry have shared during the video conference. However, it is clear that in both entities there remain doubts and unresolved issues (memorandum accounts and allowance for doubtful accounts).

6.7 The Facticity of Accrual Accounting

After all these observations are systematized during about 18 months of the trial, it is necessary to analyze all these statements adopting the Latour theory. Specifically, we follow the *facticity diagram* explained above (Fig. 5.4). During the first semester of implementation of accrual accounting (June-December 2012), various issues were discussed during the weekly video conferences. The issue less debated, just mentioned in one video conference (5th June 2012) is about the *International Public Sector Accounting Standards* (IPSAS). Specifically, it is pointed out by the consultants that the principles being drafted into the national reform are not consistent with the dictates of the international standards. This represents *a statement type 5*, because it is not questioned or argued in any way. It is not mentioned in subsequent meetings but is taken for granted. Continuing downward, it is possible to see the issue "*memorandum accounts*" that is being addressed by the academy. Indeed, there was some confusion about the meaning and usage of these accounts. They were confused with clearance accounts, which are a typical instrument of financial accounting. Professor Mussari sent a note to the implementers explaining how to use this instrument. This represents a *statement type 4*. One can recognize a *statement type 3* in the discussions around the state of completion of the work, in particular, the moment of *recognition of the cost*. Specifically, in the previous paragraphs, it is demonstrated how the technicians are rigid; they don't want to be manipulated. Indeed, the decision made by the technicians to link the cost to the commitment preserves the tradition of the commitment accounting (stabilized practice). The issues most challenged, for which we find statements type 1 and type 2 that can be likened to conjecture, are related to the depreciation (type 2) and *evaluation of assets* (type 1). In particular, the arguments are the evaluation of heritage assets and the state property assets. These issues show how accrual accounting in its implementation phase assumes the status of artifact.

During the second semester of observations (January-June 2013), it is possible to see that the most debated issues are still those that affect *the evaluation* and *the depreciation of assets*. During this period, Prof. Mussari sent a note (in March) in which he seeks to shed light on the subject. However, the statements are still *type 1* and *type 2*.

A new topic is introduced with the same lack of clarity, the *allowance for doubtful accounts*. Specifically, the technicians of Campania region declare that there is *no assurance* regarding the *reliability of these accounts*. A high level of *subjectivity* is found in discussions regarding the formation of the first balance sheet, in particular, the misunderstanding about the *Equity section*.

During the semester January-June 2013 and during the semester June-December 2013, the technicians also address issues related to the recording accounting method. They refer to the double-entry bookkeeping. On this topic that is completely unknown, they made numerous machinations, specifically; they presented and shared examples of records on typical management operations. So starting from the criteria (evaluation of assets, the arise of cost) by way of the recording activity until the formation of the first balance sheet, it is clear that the way in which the local translators interpret these issues reveal the subjectivity of accrual accounting and its status as an artifact (Fig. 6.5).

Finally, in order to answer the questions posed at the beginning of this chapter, it is possible to say that the accrual accounting does not affect a sufficiently large number of actors to combine forces in a convergent manner. As a consequence, its translation does not appear to be sufficiently linear. In almost all the stories reported in this chapter, it is evident that accrual accounting, once entered in the action net of the laboratory (the local translation center) takes on other meanings, follows different trajectories and never has a stable identity. Indeed, among human actors (consultants and academics, technicians of other entities) and non-human actors (the national standard), the different trajectories of its translations are never linear. In every video conference, there are forces which drive implementers to abandon the previous path for a new one. It is explicit that these deviations, come from defects within the starting components of the technology, contained in the policy of its constructions.

Thus, comprehensively analyzing these results, it is clear that the way in which the local translators interpret, borrow, these issues, reveals the subjectivity of accrual accounting and its status as an artifact. The artifact is related to different reasons: the process of self-reform which arises in a trial that contributes to the distortions; that is why, the rules imposed by decree, which in some parts is incomprehensible, are not very adaptable to the dynamics of the public entities; the translation appears as a reworking of the traditional accounting system known in the private sector, where there are continuous interventions, often in its fundamental aspects, such as the matching principle of an accrual accounting system.

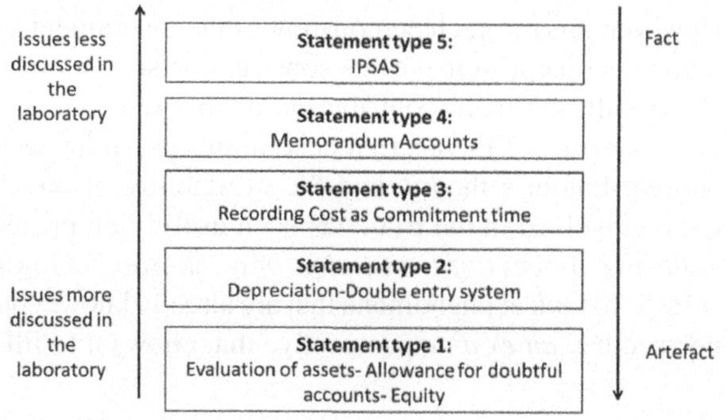

Fig. 6.5 The facticity diagram of accrual accounting

Specifically, in this chapter, it has been shown the "*action net*" (Gherardi & Lippi, 2000, p. 151) in the laboratory; it has been identified *four types of actors* that precede and implement translation, respectively,

- *consultants and academics* who *produced knowledge*;
- *politicians*, those that *govern the process*, from the input stage of the decree;
- *technical and political Committees* those occurred in the process, which is involved in the input stage as well;
- the *technicians*, civil servants, those who actively put it into practice.

All these actors have differently influenced the laboratory life in Campania region, as the various players in a rugby game, some of them decided in the first instance the trajectory, others have changed it, bringing it forward or interrupting it.

Finally, the restricted knowledge about the "black box accrual accounting" reveals that it is still a fluid object and relatively stable. The uncertainties and doubts surrounding the accrual accounting in public sector are many. These unclear areas are not entirely dissipated and remain after the translation. Overall, there is a large group of administrators who resist translating accrual accounting systems into the public domain for two main reasons: uncertainty about its identity and its usefulness; other measures contained in the reform, other black boxes, must be implemented and perceived as priorities.

6.8 Conclusion

In New Public Management, accrual accounting is considered useful in evaluating government performance in terms of service cost and efficiency(Guthrie, 1998). The accrual basis may also enhance cash flow information and provide other financial information, which may be useful in assessing the financial position of government entities (Hyndman & Connolly, 2011). It is suggested that accrual accounting may benefit users by giving them better information for decision-making and accountability. It may also change the way managers think and operate (Likierman, 1992). However, this research demonstrates that government adoption of accrual accounting without a blueprint makes its construction so complicated as to be a *fabrication*.

Overall, the main contribution of this research is to make evident the artifacts that characterize the accrual accounting in public sector. The theoretical approach chosen, Latour's theory, and the availability of data, the direct observations in a region involved in the trial, has been useful in representing the reform process as a *collective process of translation in a laboratory*. In other words, the scope of this study is to look at phenomena that are already known, but to do so adopting a different perspective: *an ex ante* perspective that allows it to fill gaps in the literature.

In particular, this research has clearly shown:

- the *non-linearity* of the policy's path, in the input stage and in its implementation phase;
- the *artifacts* that characterize the accrual accounting in public sector, which became visible opening the *black box* and the study of the *science in the making* instead of science already made;
- *policy* is studied *as a blueprint*; the accrual accounting system is studied *as a new technology* to be built. The *trial* does not represent just a bottom-up process but *is also a collective process of construction.*

In spite of the vision that describes accrual accounting as a system that is fully integrated into the organization, this study shows that it is not anchored to the same extent in the public sector realities, in this specific case, in the regional reality. Thus, beyond the apparent objectivity and neutrality of facts, the way in which local actors arise in connection with the artifacts, interpreting and appropriating them, demonstrates the *subjectivity* and the *non-neutrality* of accrual accounting.

Considering the research questions: "What is accrual accounting for governments?" "Is it a *neutral technology* in the hands of rationale decision makers?" The answear is: "No, it is not". The process does not appear to be fluid, but rather is messy and confused". The initial analysis is focused on policy document analysis. It reveals the dynamic of translations of interest between policy-makers. This aspect offers reflections over a particular dimension, the meaning and the motivation behind the introduction of accrual accounting in both the policy and the way that governments' shape and follow their reforms.

From the document analysis, it is evident that this policy is not a blueprint and the case study analysis confirms that it makes slight changes to its construction. Thus, there is not a blueprint. Accrual accounting is not neutral because there is *subjectivity, interpretation*, and *fabrication.* The evidence from the "intricate novel" of documented policies and data collected about accrual accounting showed us that there is not a conceptual framework that prescribes the "meaning" of accrual accounting in terms of its scope, its objective, and its limits.

In the results chapter, it is evident how *"informal" communication* became *rules.* It derives this information from weekly video conference calls organized with those responsible for experimentation in the regions. These conferences arose spontaneously based on the needs of the leaders in the four regions, which are undertaking the experiments. It is a well-established methodology, necessary for sharing good practice. During 2012 and 2013, the first and the second year of the trial, the laboratory's analysis revealed interesting constructions. However, it becomes clear that there is a need for those responsible for the trial to communicate and share doubts. These doubts arise from confusing rules. The evidence reveals that a "messy process" is enacted, specifically in central government. Specifically, this research explains the contrast between *subjectivity, artifact*, and *objectivity, the fact.* Accrual accounting, which in most of the NPM literature is assumed as self-evident tool with the *meaning, role* and *function, durability* and *immutability* from original project, taken for granted, in this study this is questioned going back to disputes of its construction, opening the black box, starting from its original plan, the blueprint. So some authors in previous researches have already demonstrated the *subjectivity* (Hyndman & Connolly, 2011), the *non-neutrality* (Christiaens & Van Peteghem, 2007), and the *ambiguity* (Arnaboldi & Lapsley, 2009) of accrual accounting; in this research, it has been opened the black box, highlighting the machinations in the social process of its constructions. In particular, problematic aspects arose from some technical issues, including the interpretation and fabrications related to the shaping of the standard, the identification of administrative phenomena on an accrual basis, the introduction of new procedures to carry out the process, and the adaptation of the structure for managing the flow of new information.

In the Italian reform, the accrual accounting has been depicted an instrument "for cognitive purpose", i.e., raising awareness rather than inspiring management to take action. This role is intended to increase its awareness within public management and is included in a reform for the harmonization of public sector accounting in public administration. It should be the instrument that shapes consolidated financial statements. However, the evidence from non-participant observations reveals that the formal decision to adopt accrual accounting for government bodies is not enough to ensure that this policy is actually implemented.

The Campania region, after Decree 118/2011 on public sector harmonization reform, adhered to the trial which is still ongoing. As a consequence, the entity has agreed to apply the new accounting principles and to introduce the accrual accounting system into its reporting system and, to prepare for the first time, a new version of the balance sheet. The analysis of the video conferences shows that the Campania region started by recognizing the rules contained in the policy in an effort to understand what information was relevant to the proper implementation of accrual accounting. In this recognition process, there were many divergences from the original path. For example, it became clear that it was difficult to implement the evaluation of assets. Considered the country's institutional structure, it is necessary to say that Italian Regions have their own accounting laws. In the past, the Italian regions were not required to prepare financial statements based on accrual accounting principles. The Campania region, on the basis of the regional Law n. 19 of 2009, drew up a building-heritage statement based on established practice. It contains information regarding the size, the area, the location, etc.; however, there is no information regarding depreciation, net value, and any other accounting information. From the video conference call, it is evident that the accrual principle in construction is not completely related to the rule of Civil Code for private companies, nor does it abide by principles provided by the local governments. Thus, those responsible for the trial in the Campania Region included consultants, technicians from the offices of state property, requested the involvement of an academic, expert in public sector accounting. However, there is not a unique or shared solution, and many interpretations were presented.

The main limitation of this study is related to the partial result focused on the first phase of the policy (input) and in the second phase (the implementation) the *problematization* phase (Gherardi & Lippi, 2000; Latour, 1987), which considers the managerial implications of these findings for policy-makers, after 18 months of trial. An interesting aspect is (Gherardi & Lippi, 2000; Latour, 1987) evaluating the outcome of the policy and the two main risks related to accrual accounting reform: the *stalled implementation*, or whether this will *become a mere formal tool*. In other words analyze if the main actors involved in this reform are or not able to confirm with certainty that accrual accounting is in operation. The fragility of the results could be fulfilled with an extension of this research, with a next stage of investigation to analyze the system in operation.

Finally, it would also be interesting to conduct similar studies in other European country where a similar reform has already been or is going to be implemented. This will make it possible to initiate an international debate.

Glossary

Artifact An *artifact* or *artefact* (from Latin phrase *arte factum*, from *ars* skill + *facere* to make) is *something made or given shape by man*, such as a tool or a work of art. For example, this might include an object of archaeological interest. Artifact is the only spelling in North American English, but other English-speaking countries also accept *artefact*. The artifacts assume a project, a purpose, and therefore, a type of intelligence capable of creative activity.

Blueprint A blueprint is a reproduction of a technical drawing, documenting architecture or an engineering design, using a contact-print process on light-sensitive sheets. Introduced in the nineteenth century, the process allowed rapid and accurate reproduction of documents used in construction and industry.

Cadavre exquis This is a game that collectively assembles a collection of words or images. Each collaborator adds to a composition in sequence. The technique was invented by Surrealists.

Construction This is a building process that starts from a project's conception through the physical construction of a system.

(To) Define To determine the boundary or extent of; (often passive) to delineate the form or outline of. The shape of the tree was clearly defined by the light behind it. An object is defined by the behavior shown in laboratory tests.

Devices These are artifices by means of which all traces of construction technology at some point become difficult to discover and recognize.

Experiment Is a *story,* is an *event*, is an *action*, is a *text* about non-textual situation.

Experimentation Experts, equipped with instruments to follow *the collective experiment* in a controlled environment.

Fabrication A construction process that involves subjective interpretation.

Fact In philosophy, the concept fact is considered in epistemology and ontology. Questions of objectivity and truth are closely associated with questions of fact.

Inception The beginning of something, such as an undertaking; a commencement.

Laboratory Is a facility that provides controlled conditions in which scientific or technological research, experiments, and measurement may be performed. According to Latour, in the laboratories are defined objects, technologies.

A. Bruno, *New Public Management (NPM) and the Introduction of an Accrual Accounting System*, SpringerBriefs in Accounting,
https://doi.org/10.1007/978-3-030-57386-7

Modalities The operating procedures, the accounting proposals, and resolutions (book-keeping records, the accounting evaluation), which are continuously integrated, edited, reversed, and deleted.

Pandora's Box Pandora's Box is an artifact in Greek mythology, taken from the myth of Pandora's creation in Hesiod's Works and Days. The "box" was actually a large jar (πίθοςpithos) given to Pandora (Πανδώρα, "all-gifted", "all-giving"), which contained all the evils of the world. In this research, this concept refers to Latour's theory (Latour, 1999).

Translation A geometric shift from one phase to another or the process of translating words or text from one language into another. In this research, this concept refers to Callon's theory (Callon, 1986).

Script In computer science, it refers to a particular type of program, specifically a particular written programming language, the interpreted language. Thus, the script is a particular computer program defined as "command line interpreter". The terms are command-line interpreter or command language interpreter. In this study, it is adopted this perspective "the script is embedded in artifacts, because they influence the behavior of the users" (Panozzo, 2000, p. 115).

References

Akrich, M. (1992). The de-scription of technical objects. In W. Bijker & J. Law (Eds.), *A cura di shaping technology-building society* (pp. 205–224). Cambridge: Mit Press.

Anessi Pessina, E. (2012). L'esperienza della contabilità economico patrimoniale nella sanità. In F. Capalbo (Ed.), *A cura di L'applicazione della contabiltà economica nel settore pubblico: Aspettative, risultati e criticità* (pp. 100–128). Torino: Giappichelli.

Anessi Pessina, E. (2007). *L'evoluzione dei sistemi contabili pubblici.* Egea: Milano.

Anselmi, L., Pavan, A., & Reginato, E. (2012). Cassa, competenza finanziaria e competenza economica: La scelta delle basi contabili in un sistema armonizzato di contabilità pubblica. *Azienda Pubblica, 25*(1), 53–68.

Anselmi, L., & Ponzo, S. (2009). *Critical issues in reforming public sector accounting: Problems of transition to accrual accounting and first time implementation of IPSAS's.* Paper presented in Modena to the 12th Biennal Cigar Conference.

Arnaboldi, M., & Lapsley, I. (2009). On the implementation of accrual accounting: A study of conflict and ambiguity. *European Accounting Review*, (18)(4), 809–836.

Bachelard, G. (2007). *Studi di filosofia della scienza.* Collana epistemologia, Milano: Mimemis.

Barton, A. (1999). Public and private sector accounting–the non identical twins. *Australian Accounting Review, 9*(2), 22–31.

Benito, B., Brusca, I., & Montesinos, V. (2007). The harmonization of government financial information systems: The role of the IPSASs. *International Review of Administrative Sciences, 73*(2), 293–317.

Bijker, W. (1995). *Of Bicycles, Bakelites and bulbs: Toward a theory of sociotechnical change.* Cambridge: MIT Press.

Bisogno, M. (2008). I sistemi contabili del settore pubblico nell'esperienza italiana. In A. Tommasetti, *A cura di I sistemi contabili nelle amministrazioni pubbliche una prospettiva internazionale* (pp. 39–130). Padova: Cedam.

Borgonovi, E. (2005). Cambiamento e riforme nelle regioni italiane. *Azienda Pubblica, 18*(1), 5–9.

Briers, M., & Chua, W. F. (2001). The role of actor-networks and boundary objects in management accounting change: A field study of an implementation of activity-based costing. *Accounting, Organizations and Society, 26*, 237–269.

Broadbent, J., & Guthrie, J. (2008). Public sector to public services: 20 years of "contextual" accounting research. *Accounting, Auditing & Accountability Journal, 21*(2), 129–169.

Bruno, A. (2014). Harmonizing budgeting and accounting: The case of Italy. *Open Journal of Accounting, 3*, 38–44.

Bruno, A. (2013). Lo stato dell'arte della sperimentazione in Regione Campania. *Finanza Locale, 5–6*, 43–51.

A. Bruno, *New Public Management (NPM) and the Introduction of an Accrual Accounting System*, SpringerBriefs in Accounting,
https://doi.org/10.1007/978-3-030-57386-7

Bruno, A., & Lapsley, I. (2018). The emergence of an accounting practice: The fabrication of a government accrual accounting system. *Accounting, Auditing & Accountability Journal, 31*(4) (in the Special Forum Section on 'Doings of practitioners: public sector accountants in the 21st Century').

Burns, J., & Scapens, R. (2000). Conceptualizing management accounting change: An institutional framework. *Mangement Accounting Research, 11*, 3–25.

Caccia, L., & Steccolini, I. (2006). Accounting change in Italian local governments: What's beyond managerial. *Critical Perspectives on Accounting, 17*(2–3), 154–174.

Callon, M. (1986). Some elements of a sociology of translation: Domestication of the scallops and the fishermen. In *Power, action and belief: A new sociology of knowledge?* (pp. 196–223). London: Routledge.

Cañibano, L., & Mora, A. (2000). Evaluating the statistical significance of "de facto" accounting harmonization: A study of European global players. *European Accounting Review, 9*(3), 349–370.

Caperchione, E. (2003). Local government accounting system reform in Italy: A critical analysis. *Journal of Public Budgeting, Accounting and Financial Management, 15*(1), 110–145.

Caperchione, E. (2008). Tendenze in atto nel rinnovamento del sistema informativo-contabile delle Regioni. In F. Pezzani, *A cura di Ripensare il ruolo e la governance delle Regioni* (pp. 7–22). Milano: Egea.

Caperchione, E. (2012). L'armonizzazione contabile nella prospettiva internazionale. *Azienda Pubblica, 25*(1), 83–99.

Carnegie, G., & Wolnizer, P. (1996). Enabling accountability in Museums. *Accounting, Auditing and Accountability Journal, 9*(5), 84–99.

Carosi, A. (2012). Introduzione. In F. Capalbo, *A cura di L'applicazione della contabilità economica nel settore pubblico: Aspettative, risultati e criticità* (pp. 5–11).Torino: Giappichelli.

Chan, J. (2003). Government accounting: An assessment of theory, purpose and standards. *Public, Money & Mangement, 23*(1), 13–20.

Christensen, M., & Skaerbaek, P. (2010). Consultancy output and purification of accounting technologies. *Accounting, Organization and Society, 35*(5), 524–545.

Christensen, M., & Parker, L. (2010). Using Ideas to advances professions: Public sector accrual accounting. *Financial Accountability and Management, 26*(3), 246–264.

Christiaens, J., & Reyniers, B. (2009). Impact of IPSAS on Reforming governmental financial information systems: A comparative study. *Working paper*, University of Gent (pp. 1–17).

Christiaens, J., & Van Peteghem, V. (2007). Governmental accounting reform: Evolution of the implementation in Flemish municipalities. *Financial Accoutability and Management, 23*(4), 375–399.

Clarke, F. (2012). The use and abuse of accrual accounting in the public sector. In F. Capalbo, *A cura di L'applicazione della contabilità economica nel settore pubblico: Aspettative, risultati e criticità* (pp. 3–26). Torino: Giappichelli.

Connolly, C., & Hyndman, N. (2006). The actual implementation of accrual accounting: Caveats from a case within the UK public sector. *Accounting, Auditing and Accountability Journal, 19*(2), 272–290.

D'Alessio, L. (2012). Logiche e criteri di armonizzazione nelle recenti normative di riforma della contabilità pubblica. *Azienda Pubblica, 25*(1), 23–39.

Dean, G., & Pilcher, R. (2012). The consequence of accrual reporting on local government risk-australian evidence. In F. Capalbo (Ed.), *A cura di L'applicazione della contabilità economica nel settore pubblico: Aspettative, risulatati e criticità* (pp. 27–48).Torino: Giappichelli.

Di Pietra, R. (2000). *Ragioneria Internazionale e "armonia" contabile*. Padova: Cedam.

Evans, J., & Patton, J. (1987). Signaling and monitoring in public-sector accounting. *Journal of Accounting Research, 25*, 130–158.

Gherardi, S., & Lippi, A. (2000). *Tradurre le riforme in pratica*. Milano: Raffaello Cortina Editore.

Guthrie, J. (1998). Application of accrual accounting in the Australian public sector: Rethoric or reality. *Financial Accountabiliy & Management, 14*(1), 1–19.

Godfrey, A., Devlin, P., & Merrouche, C. (2001). A diffusion-contingency model for government accounting innovations. *International Comparative Issues in Government Accounting*, 279–296.

Hines, R. (1988). Financial accounting: In communicating reality, we construct reality. *Accounting, Organizations and Society, 13*(3), 251–262.

Hoffman, E. (1997). Public Choice Experiments. In D. Mueller (Ed.), *A cura di perspectives on public choice* (pp. 415–426). Cambridge: Cambridge University Press.

Hood, C. (1991). A public management for all season. *Public Administration, 69*(1), 3–19.

Hood, C. (1995). The "new public management" in the 1980s: Variations on a theme. *Accounting, Organizations and Society, 20*, 93–109.

Hyndman, N., & Connolly, C. (2011). Accruals Accounting in the public sector: A road not always taken. *Management Accounting Research, 22*, 36–45.

Innes, J., & Mitchell, F. (1990). The process of change in management: Some field study evidence. *Management Accounting Research, 1*, 3–19.

Jagalla, T., Becker, S., & Weber, J. (2011). A taxonomy of perceived benefits of accrual accounting and budgeting: Evidence from German states. *Financial Accountability & Management, 27*(2), 134–165.

Jannelli, R. (2012). Le garanzie offerte dalla revisione nei sistemi di contabilità economica. In F. Capalbo (Ed.), *A cura di L'applicazione della contabilità economica nel settore pubblico: Aspettative, risultati e criticità* (pp. 243–268). Torino: Giappichelli.

Joannidès, V., & Berland, N. (2013). Constructing a research network: Accounting knowledge in production. *Accounting, Auditing & Accountability Journal, 26*(4), 512–538.

Kasurinen, T. (2002). Exploring management accounting change: The case of balanced scorecard implementation. *Management Accounting Research*, 323–343.

Lapsley, I. (1999). Accounting and the new public management: Instruments of substantive efficiency or a rationalising modernity? *Financial Accountability and Management, 15*(3–4), 201–207.

Lapsley, I. (2012). Accounting mutations: Accrual accounting in the UK public sector. In F. Capalbo (Ed.), *A cura di accrual accounting in public administration: International experiences* (pp. 49–63). Milano: Giuffrè.

Lapsley, I., & Pallot, J. (2000). Accounting, management and organizational change: A comparative study of local government. *Management Accounting Research, 11*, 213–229.

Lapsley, I., & Wright, E. (2004). The diffusion of management accounting innovations. *Management Accounting Research, 15*(3), 355–374.

Lapsley, I., Mussari, R., & Paulsson, G. (2009). On the adoption of accrual accounting in the public sector: A self-evident and problematic reform. *European Accounting Review, 18*(4), 719–723.

Latour, B. (1987). *Science in action: How to follow scientists and engineers through society.* Cambridge: Harvard University Press.

Latour, B. (2011). *Hybrid thoughts in a hibrid world.* Great Britain: CPI Antony Rowe, Chippenham, Wiltshire.

Latour, B. (1988). *The pasteurization of France.* Cambridge, MA: Harward UP.

Latour, B. (1993). *We have never been modern.* Cambridge: Cambridge University Press.

Latour, B. (1999). *Pandora's hope essays in the reality of science studies.* London: Harvard University Press.

Latour, B. (2002). Morality and technology: The end of the means. *Theory Culture and Society, 19*(5–6), 247–260.

Latour, B. (2013). *Cogitamus Sei lettere sull'umanesimo scientifico.* Bologna: il Mulino.

Latour, B., & Ewald, F. (2008). *Disinventare la modernità. Conversazioni con François Ewald.* Milano: Eleuthera .

Latour, B., & Woolgar, S. (1979, 1986). *Laboratory life, the social Construction of scientific facts.* London: Sage Library of Social Research.

Levi, R., & Valverde, M. (2008). Studying law by association: Bruno Latour goes to the Conseil d'État. *Law & Social Inquiry, 33*(3), 805–825.

Likierman, A. (1992). Financial reporting in the public sector. In D. Henry & C. Holtman, *A cura di public sector accounting and financial control*. London: Chapman & Hall.

Luckhurst, R. (2006). Bruno Latour's scientification: Networks, assemblages and tangled objects. *Science Fiction Studies, 33*, 4–17.

Lüder, K. (1992). A contingency model of governmental accounting innovations in the political-administrative environment. *Reserach in Governmental and Nonprofit Accounting, 7*, 99–127.

Lüder, K., & Jones, R. (2003). Reforming Governmental accounting and budgeting in Europe. Price Waterhouse Coopers.

Mautz, R. (1988) (editorial). *Monuments, mistakes and opportunities. Accounting Horizons* (pp. 123–128).

Meneguzzo, M., Jannelli, R., Rossi, N., & Tesone, C. (2013). *Many Report, a storm of laws and few accountability: Rethinking public sector accounting in Italy.* Paper presented in Salerno, EGPA Conference, University of Salerno.

Miller, P. (1991). Accounting innovation beyond the enterprise: Problematizing investment decisions and programming economic growth in the UK in the 1960s. *Accounting Organizations and Society, 16*(8), 733–762.

Miller, P., & O' Leary, T. (1987). The accounting and the construction of the Governable Person. *Accounting, Organizations and Society*, 1–31.

Miller, G. (1997). Contextualizing texts: Studying organizational texts. In G. Miller & R. Dingwall (Eds.), *A cura di context and method in qualitative research* (pp. 77–91). London: Sage.

Miller, F. A., & Alvarado, K. (2005). Incorporating documents into qualitative nursing research. *Journal of Nursing Scholarship, 37*(4), 348–353.

Miller, P. (1998). The margins of accounting. *The European Accounting Review, 7*(4), 605–621.

Miller, P. (2001). Governing by numbers: Why calculative practices matter. *Social Research, 68*(2), 379–396.

Mosse, D. (2004). Is good policy unimplementable? Reflections on the ethnography of aid policy and practice? *Development and Change, 35*(4), 639–671.

Mueller, D. (2008). Public choice: An introduction. In C. Rowely & F. Schneider, *A cura di Readings in Public Choice and Constitutional Political Economy* (pp. 31–45). Charlottenburg: Springer Science.

Mussari, R. (1995). Italian local government reform: An application of professor lüder's contingency model, Paper presented at the 6th CIGAR Conference, Paris.s.n.

Mussari, R. (2012). Brevi considerazioni sui mutamenti in atto nei sistemi si contabilità pubblica. *Azienda Pubblica, 25*(1), 11–21.

Mussari, R., Grossi, G., & Castelnuovo, A. (2005). Italy. *Reforming governmental accounting and budgeting in Europe* (pp. 391–579). Frankfurter Straße: Fachverlag Moderne Wirtschaft.

Nasi, G., & Steccolini, I. (2008). Implementation of acconting reform: An empirical investigation into Italian local governments. *Public Management Review, 10*(2), 175–196.

Nesbakk, L. G., & Mellemvik, F. (2011). The construction of materiality in government accounting: A case of constraining factors and the difficulties of hybridization. *Financial Accountability and Management, 27*(2), 195–214.

Newberry, S. (2012). The use of accrual accounting in New Zealand's Central Government: Achievements and Second Thoughts. In F. Capalbo (Ed.), *A cura di L'applicazione della contabilità economica nel settore pubblico: Aspettative, risultati e criticità* (pp. 65–70). Torino: Giappichelli.

Newberry, S., & Pallot, J. (2005). A wolf in sheep's clothing? Wider consequences of the financial management system of the New Zealand central government. *Financial Accountability & Management, 21*(3), 263–277.

Olson, O., Guthrie, J., & Humphrey, C. (1998). *Global warning! Debating international developments in new public financial mangement*. Oslo: Cappelen Akademisk Forlag.

Otley, D. (1980). The contingencytheory of management accounting: Achievement and prognosis. *Accounting, Organizations and Society, 5*(4), 413–428.

Panozzo, F. (2000). L'ingegneria dell'eterogeno ovvero la fabbricazione del controllo di gestione. In S. Gherardi & A. Lippi (Eds.), *A cura di Tradurre le riforme in pratica* (pp. 115–147). Milano: Raffaele Cortina Editore.

Pettigrew, A. (1997). What is a processual analysis. *Scandinavian Journal of Management, 13*(4), 337–348.

Patton, M. (2002). Qualitative research & evaluation methods. 3rd a cura di Thousand Oaks, CA: Sage.

Pezzani, F. (2008). *Ripensare il ruolo e la governance delle Regioni.* Milano: Egea.

Pina, V., Torres, L., & Yetano, A. (2009). Accrual accounting in EU local governments: One method several approaches. *European Accounting Review, 18*(4), 765–807.

Powell, W., & Di Maggio, P. (1983). The iron cage revisited: Institutional isomorphism and collective rationality. *American Sociological Review, 48,* 147–160.

Potito, L. (1973). *I principi contabili generalmente accettati.* Napoli: Giannini.

Pozzoli, S. (2012). Un processo di armonizzazione che mortifica la contabilità pubblica. *Azienda Pubblica, 25*(1), 69–82.

Pratt, M. G. (2008). Fitting oval pegs into round holes. *Organizational Research Method, 11*(3), 481–509.

Preston, A., Cooper, D., & Coombs, R. W. (1992). Fabricating Budgets: A study of the production of management budgeting in the national health service. *Accounting Organizations and Society, 17*(6), 561–593.

Quattrone, P. (2009). Books to be practiced: Memory, the power of the visual, and the success of accounting. *Accounting, Organizations and Society, 34*(1), 85–118.

Ricci, P. (2005). *Enti strumentali regionali e loro accountability. Il caso Campania.* Roma: FrancoAngeli.

Ricci, P. (2012a). Il potenziale impatto delle nuove disposizioni contabili sui comportamenti aziendali e sul sistema economico. *Azienda Pubblica, 25*(1), 41–52.

Ricci, P. (2012b). *Riformite.* Rimini: Maggioi Editore.

Robson, K. (1992). Accounting numbers as "inscription": Action at a distance and the development of accounting. *Accounting, Organisations and Society, 17*(7), 685–708.

Ryan, C. (1998). The introduction of accrual reporting policy in the Australian public sector–an agenda setting explanation. *Accounting, Auditing & Accountability Journal, 11*(5), 518–539.

Saleh, Z., & Pendlebury, M. (2006). Accruals accounting in government developments in Malaysia. *Asia Pacific Business Review*, 421–435.

Steccolini, I. (2009). *Cambiamenti e innovazioni nei sistemi contabili pubblici. Determinanti, ciriticità, prospettive.* Milano: Egea.

Ter Bogt, H. J., & Van Helden, G. J. (2000). Accounting Change in Dutch Government: Exploring the Gap between Expectations and Realisations. *Management Accounting Research, 11*(2).

Upping, P., & Oliver, J. (2011). Accounting change model for the public sector: Adapting Luder's model for developing countries. *International Review of Business Research Papers,* 364–380.

Van Der Tas, L., Raffournier, B., Haller, A., & Walter, P. (1992). Measuring International harmonization and standardization: A comment. *Abacus, 28*(2), 211–216.

Winner, L. (1986). *Do artifacts have politics?* Chicago: University of Chicago Press.

Yamamoto, K. (1999). Accounting system reform in Japanese local governments. *Financial Accountability and Management,* 291–307.

Yin, R. (2009). *Case study Research Design and Methods.* London: Sage Ltd.

Normative References and On-Line Source

Allegato 3 DPCM 28 dicembre 2011, *Arconet-Armonizzazione contabile enti territoriali.* https://www.rgs.mef.gov.it/VERSIONE-I/eGOVERNME1/ARCONET/Sperimentazione/.

Corte dei Conti, *Audizione sullo schema di d.lgs. n. 339 recante disposizioni per l'attuazione dell'articolo 2, comma 2, lettera h) della legge 5 maggio 2009, n. 42 e successive modificazioni.*https://www.corteconti.it/export/sites/portalecdc/_documenti/chi_siamo/audizioni/audizione_17_maggio_2011.pdf.
CIVIT, 2012, *Rapporto Civit, Commissione per l'integrità e la valutazione delle amministrazioni pubbliche.* https://www.civit.it/wp-content/uploads/Delibera-n.-2.2012.pdf.
Conferenza Stato-Regioni. (2011). *Report della Conferenza Unificata del 3 marzo 2011.* https://www.statoregioni.it/dettaglioDoc.asp?idprov=12822&iddoc=43253&tipodoc=5&CONF=UNI.
Copaff. (2011). *Verbale del 24 maggio 2011 della Commissione Parlamentare per l'attuazione del federalismo fiscale.* https://www.camera.it/_dati/leg16/lavori/stenbic/6205/2011/0524/INTERO.pdf.
Copaff. (2011). *Verbale della Commissione per l'attuazione del federalismo fiscale dell'8 giugno 2011.* https://parlamento.camera.it/organismi_bicamerali/16/128/131/135/scheda_commissione.asp?tipo_ricerca=anno_mese&nmese=6&nanno=2011&mostra=Mostra+elenco.
Copaff. (2011). *Verbale della Commissione per l'attuazione del federalismo fiscalede del 1° giugno 2011.* https://parlamento.camera.it/organismi_bicamerali/16/128/131/135/scheda_commissione.asp?tipo_ricerca=anno_mese&nmese=6&nanno=2011&mostra=Mostra+elenco.
Ernst & Young. (2012). *Overview and comparison of public accounting and auditing practices in the 27 EU Member States.* https://epp.eurostat.ec.europa.eu/portal/page/portal/government_finance_statistics/documents/study_on_public_accounting_and_auditing_2012.pdf.
Ministro dell'Economia e delle Finanze Saccomanni. (23 maggio 2013). *Relazione sui risultati della sperimentazione dell'attuazione del decreto legislativo recante disposizioni in materia di armonizzazione dei sistemi contabili e degli schemi di bilancio delle regioni, degli enti locali e dei loro oganismi.* https://www.rgs.mef.gov.it/VERSIONE-I/e-GOVERNME1/ARCONET/Documentazione/.
OCSE. (2013). *Studi Economici dell'OCSE Italia Overview.* www.oecd.org/bookshop: OECD.
Senato della Reppublica. (2011). *Atto 359, n. 47, Schema di decreto legislativo recante disposizioni in materia di adeguamento e armonizzazione dei sistemi contabili.* https://www.senato.it/leg/16/BGT/Schede/docnonleg/21124.htm.

Internal Documents

Mussari, R. (2012). *Breve nota su conti d'ordine e partite di giro.*
Mussari, R. (2013). *Appunto del Prof. Mussari.*
Report video conferenza, 26/03/2014. *Video conferenza del 26/03/2014,* s.l.: s.n.
Report di video conferenza, 18/03/2013. *Videoconferenza del 18/03/2013,* s.l.: s.n.
Report di video conferenza, 29/10/2013. *Videoconferenza del 29/10/2013,* s.l.: s.n.
Report gruppo di lavoro, 14/01/2013. *Videoconferenza,* s.l.: s.n.
Report gruppo di lavoro, 10/07/2012. *Videoconferenza,* s.l.: s.n.
Report gruppo di lavoro, 10/12/2012. *Videoconferenza,* s.l.: s.n.
Report gruppo di lavoro, 12/11/2012. *Videoconferenza,* s.l.: s.n.
Report gruppo di lavoro, 21/01/2013. *Videoconferenza,* s.l.: s.n.
Report gruppo di lavoro, 22/10/2012. *Videoconferenza,* s.l.: s.n
Report gruppo di lavoro, 26/06/2012. *Video conferenza,* s.l.: s.n.
Report gruppo di lavoro, 27/07/2012. *Videoconferenza,* s.l.: s.n.
Report gruppo di lavoro, 3/12/2012. *Videconferenza,* s.l.: s.n.
Report Gruppo di Lavoro, 30/10/2012. *Video Conferenza,* s.l.: s.n.
Report gruppo di lavoro, 30/11/2012. *Videoconferenza,* s.l.: s.n.
Report gruppo di lavoro, 5/11/2012. *Videoconferenza,* s.l.: s.n.
Report video conferenza, 11/03/2013. *Videoconferenza 11/03/2013,* s.l.: s.n.
Report video conferenza, 2/07/2013. *Video conferenza del 2/07/2013,* s.l.: s.n.
Report video conferenza, 25/11/2013. *Video conferenza del 25/11/2013,* s.l.: s.n.